Ellora

Monumental Legacy

Series editor: Devangana Desai

Other Books in this series

DEVANGANA DESAI
Khajuraho

ANILA VERGHESE
Hampi

GEORGE MICHELL
Pattadakal

JOSÉ PEREIRA
Churches of Goa

Monumental Legacy

ELLORA

M.K. Dhavalikar

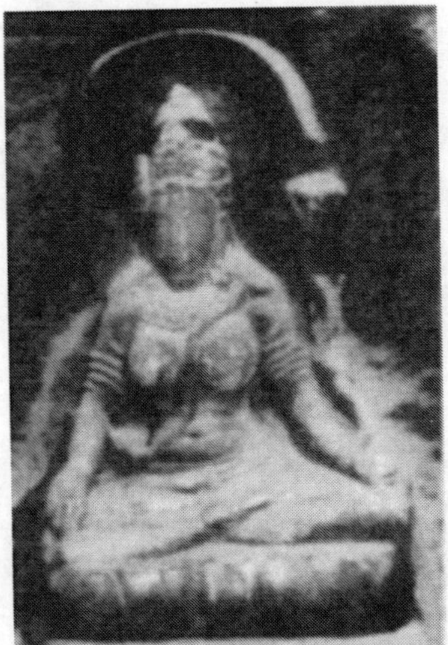

OXFORD
UNIVERSITY PRESS

OXFORD
UNIVERSITY PRESS

Oxford University Press is a department of the University of Oxford. It furthers the University's objective of excellence in research, scholarship, and education by publishing worldwide. Oxford is a registered trademark of Oxford University Press in the UK and in certain other countries

Published in India by
Oxford University Press
22 Workspace, 2nd Floor, 1/22 Asaf Ali Road, New Delhi 110002, India

First Edition published in 2003
Oxford India Paperbacks 2005
Seventh impression 2015

ISBN-13: 978-0-19-567389-0
ISBN-10: 0-19-567389-1

Typeset in Goudy
by Eleven Arts, Keshav Puram, Delhi 110 035
Printed at Manipal Technologies Limited, Manipal

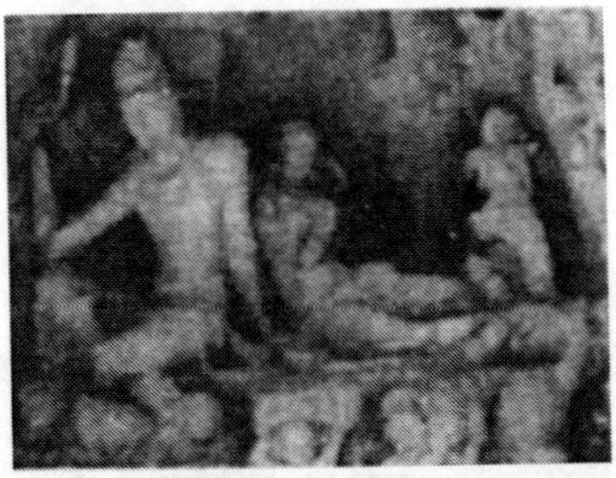

Series Editor's Preface

There are 721 sites on the World Heritage list, as on December 2001, 'inscribed' as properties by the World Heritage Committee of UNESCO. These sites are 'considered to be of outstanding value to humanity', and the preservation of this shared heritage concerns all of us. India has been an active member-state on the World Heritage Forum since 1977, and is one of the countries on the list, with 22 World Heritage Sites. Of these, 17 are recorded as cultural sites, while the rest are natural sites.

I am delighted that the Oxford University Press is publishing brief books on each of the 18 cultural sites, under its series titled *Monumental Legacy*. So far, the following cultural sites in India have been listed as World Heritage sites:

Ajanta Caves (1983), Ellora Caves (1983), Agra Fort (1983), Taj Mahal (1983), Sun Temple, Konarak (1984), Group of Monuments at Mahabalipuram (1985), Churches and Convents of Goa (1986), Group of Monuments at Khajuraho (1986), Group of Monuments at Hampi (1986), Fatehpur Sikri (1986), Group of Monuments at Pattadakal (1987), Elephanta Caves (1987), Brihadisvara Temple, Thanjavur (1987), Buddhist Monuments at Sanchi (1989),

Humayun's Tomb (1993), Qutb Minar and its Monuments (1993), the Darjeeling Himalayan Railway (1999), and Bodh Gaya (2002).

There is scope, indeed, for recognition of many more Indian sites in future on the World Heritage list. I am sure that as, and when, these are declared as World Heritage Sites, they will be included under the Monumental Legacy Series of the Oxford University Press.

The Oxford University Press, in consultation with me, has invited experts in the field to contribute small books, addressed to general readers, on each of these 17 World Heritage Sites in India. These books obviously differ from cheap tourist books and glossy guide books and, at the same time, also from specialized monographs. Their importance lies in the fact they are written by authorities on the subject, to enable visitors to see the monuments in proper perspective.

My sincere thanks to all the authors of the Series and to the editorial staff at the OUP. Their constant support and enthusiasm are much appreciated.

Devangana Desai

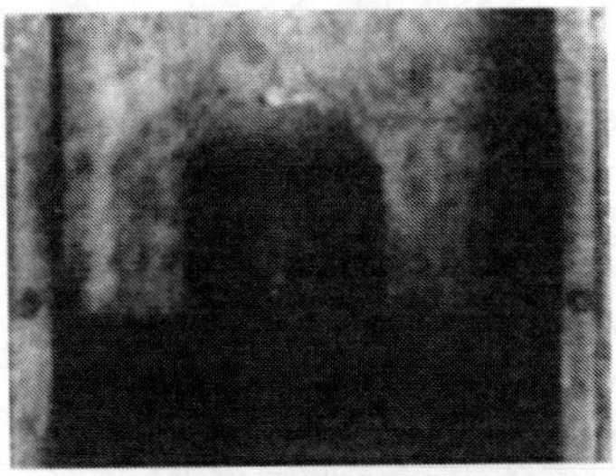

Contents

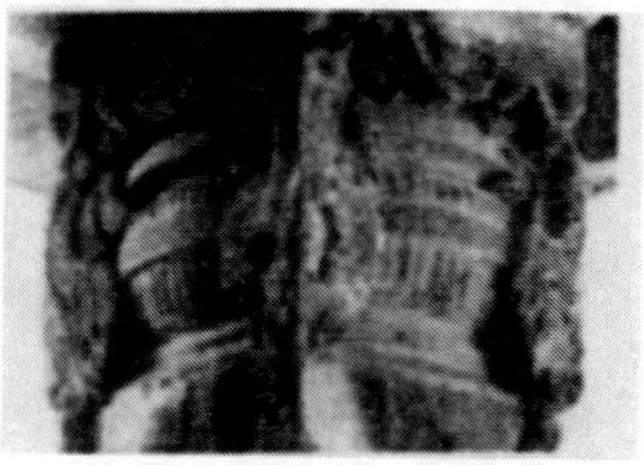

Acknowledgements

The photographs included in the book have been kindly supplied by American Institute of Indian Studies, New Delhi. The author is, therefore, grateful to Dr Pradeep Mehendiratta, Director General, American Institute of Indian Studies, New Delhi and Dr U.S. Moorti, Assistant Director, Art and Archaeology Centre (AIIS), Gurgaon. I am also thankful to Dr Suresh Vasant who read the daft and made valuable suggestions.

The map has been prepared by Shri Shrikant Pradhan, artist, Deccan College, Pune to whom my thanks are due.

M.K. Dhavalikar

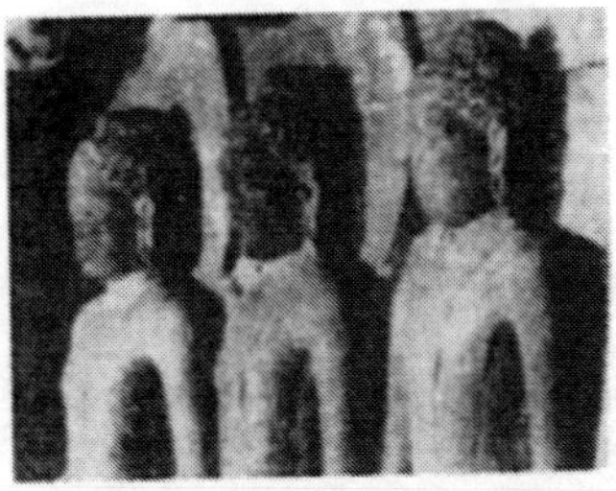

Illustrations

ONE

Development of Cave Temples in Western India

Of the 1200 rock-cut caves in India about 1000 are located in western India, more particularly in the state of Maharashtra **[Fig. 1.1]**. The region is dominated by the Sahyadri hill ranges, the basalt rock of which is ideal for carving. The Sahyadri hills lie on a north-south axis, separating the coastal region from the mainland. Its sub-ranges run mostly west-east. Caves have been excavated in these sub-ranges as well. Most of the caves are Buddhist, but there are a few Hindu and Jaina caves as well. The earliest rock-cut activity, however, began in the north, in Bihar, where caves were excavated in the Barabar and the Nagarjuni hills during the Mauryan period (third century BC). An inscription in one of the Barabar hill caves records that it was caused to be carved by king Dasharath, the grandson of Ashoka (272–32 BC) for the monks of the Ajivika sect. The rock-cut activity then shifts to western India in Maharashtra, where the caves at Bhaja were the first to be excavated in ca. 200 BC. The rock-cut idiom continued to flourish in Maharashtra till about the tenth century AD, after which structural temples came to be built on a large scale.

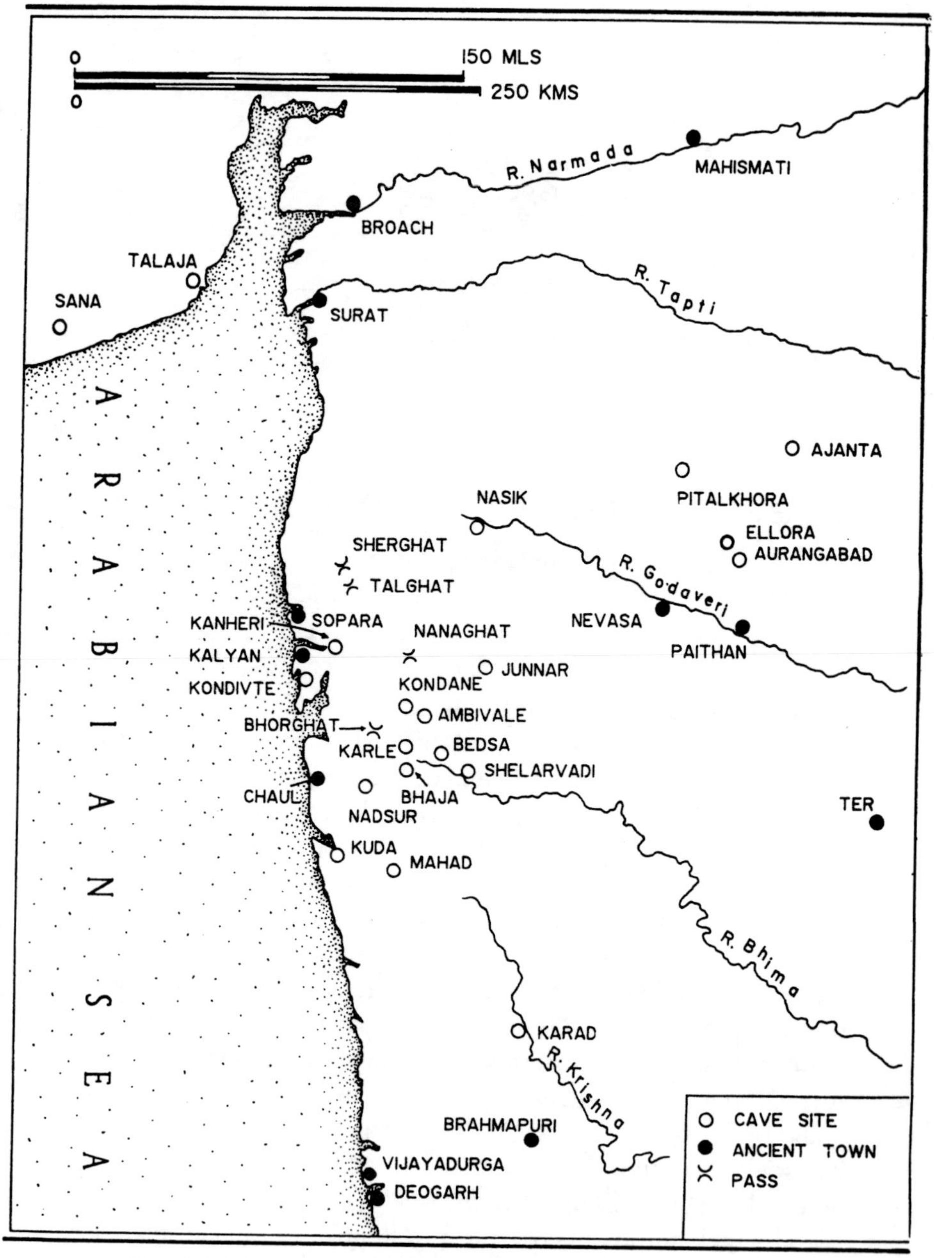

Fig. 1.1. Map of Western India showing Ellora and other cave temple sites.

The Buddhists were the first to build caves in Western India. Their caves fall into two categories; the *chaitya* or the prayer hall, which is generally apsidal on plan and is divided by a colonnade into a central nave and side aisles. The stupa in the apsidal end, which is also rock-cut, consists of a cylindrical base, with a domical top and is crowned by a squarish box-like member called *harmika*, which in turn is surmounted by a triple umbrella made of wood. When Buddha was breathing his last, he called his disciples and told them that after his death (*nirvana*), they should erect stupas over his corporeal remains at crossroads. Rock-cut stupas, which are copies of structural ones, also sometimes enshrine the relics of some venerable Buddhist monk. They are deposited in a reliquary in a small hole cut in the dome of the stupa.

The second category is *vihara*, which is generally squarish on plan with cells in the side walls and at the back, which served as the residence of the monks. Buddha had advised his monks not to stay at one place for too long and be constantly on the move. It was only during the monsoon that they had to stay at one place and hence were provided accommodation in the caves which came to be known as *vassa-vasa*, meaning 'abode during the rainy season.'

When rock-cutting activity began in western India, the artists had no previous experience of excavating caves. They were basically trained as carpenters and hence they have been referred to as carpenters working on stone. Consequently the early rock-cut caves are just copies of wooden structures in stone, and, there were numerous wooden attachments in the early caves. In fact, the chronology of early caves has been based to a considerable extent on the amount of woodwork in them. It decreased as artists gained experience in course of time.

The Buddhist rock-cutting activity in western India is divisible into two phases. In the first phase (ca. 200 BC–200 AD) the Buddha image is conspicuously absent. After a lapse of about three centuries, activity begins again and the Buddha images this time are carved. The former group belongs to the Hinayana (Lesser Vehicle) phase and the latter to the Mahayana (Greater Vehicle).

The earliest caves in western India are those at Bhaja (ca. 200 BC), situated close to the Pune–Mumbai Highway, about 65 km west of Pune near Malavali village. The main chaitya cave is apsidal on plan with a colonnade of pillars, dividing the hall into a central nave and side aisles, and has a rock-cut stupa in the apse. The facade has a simple arch and a lot of wooden attachments, of which only the holes now remain. The hall is supported by plain octagonal pillars that are not perpendicular but have an inward rake. The front pillars were also wooden. The vaulted roof is supported by wooden beams and rafters, one of which bears an inscription that says it was gifted by one Dhamabhaga.

Next in order is the Kondane chaitya, which has a facade of stone pillars. At Pitalkhora and Ajanta (Cave 10), the ribs of side aisles were cut in the rock. The Bedsa cave has an elaborate facade and the pillars have capitals with human and animal figures. The Ajanta Cave 9 is rectangular on plan and the ceiling of side aisles is flat. The Karle chaitya is most impressive with animal riders as capitals and pot bases. At Nashik, there is no wooden attachment at all.

The first phase of Buddhist caves, dated to ca. 200 BC–200 AD, belongs to the Hinayana sect, which believed in the symbolic worship of Buddha. Followers worshipped symbols such as the empty throne, foot-prints of Buddha, the pipal tree (*Ficus religiosa*) and the *triratna* (three jewels). The image of Buddha is conspicuously absent in these early caves. The first Buddha image was made in the last quarter of the first century AD in north India and it took some time to spread in different parts of the country. In western India, rock-cutting activity comes to an abrupt end from the third century AD onwards and starts again with renewed vigour from the fifth century AD, when the magnificent caves at Ajanta were excavated. They belong to the Mahayana (Greater Vehicle) faith and are characterised by the images of Buddha. After a couple of centuries, Buddhist activity comes to an end because of the decline of the religion.

The rock-cutting activity of the Hindus starts from the sixth century and the early cave temples are located in Mumbai at Jogeshwari and the nearby island of Elephanta. Excavation work in Ellora began almost at the same time. A most noteworthy feature of Hindu cave temples is that they are richly adorned with exquisite sculptures of gods and goddesses on their walls. The rock-cut art reaches its zenith in Ellora Cave 16 (Kailas), a lofty monolithic temple carved in a huge block of stone isolated from the surrounding hills. The Jainas too carved their cave temples, which are not very different in concept from their Hindu counterparts.

TWO

Historical Background

Maharashtra was inhabited by stone age man some five hundred thousand years ago, as also during the bronze age (ca. 2500–1000 BC) after which there is a hiatus upto the sixth and fifth centuries BC, which mark the beginning of the historical period in India. Ashmaka was a republican state (*Mahajanapada*) in central Maharashtra at the time of Buddha. The Asokan edicts at Sopara testify to the fact that Maharashtra was included in the Mauryan empire (fourth–second centuries BC). From the second century BC to the second century AD, it was ruled by the Satavahanas for nearly four centuries from their capital Pratishthan (Paithan, district Aurangabad). Their empire was spread over most of western and central India and Andhra, Karnataka and even the coastal region of Tamil Nadu. The early group of Buddhist caves (second century BC–second century AD) belongs to the Satavahana period, whereas those at Ajanta (later group) belong to the fifth century when the Vakatakas were ruling. During the following two centuries the region formed part of the kingdom of the Chalukyas of Badarni (Karnataka), but the next two centuries were dominated by the Rashtrakutas (ca. 750–950 AD), a major power in India, who ruled from their capitals in Maharashtra.

Elapura

The ancient name of the village was Elapura, from which the present name Verul (Marathi), and Ellora, its anglicised form, are derived. According to a Puranic account, Elapura consisted of ten settlements named after the king Ela, and that it was a *tirtha*, a sacred place. King Ela was cured of an incurable disease after he took a bath here and hence the queen decided to build a Shiva temple at the site. The name Elapura also occurs in the Chalukyan and Rashtrakuta copper plate inscriptions. The Kailas cave (No. 16) is referred to as Manakeshwar *lene* in the *Jnaneshwari* a thirteenth century Marathi commentary on the *Bhagvad-Gita*, as the *lingam* in the shrine was said to have been covered with rubies by a Rashtrakuta king in the eighth century. Chakradhar Swami, the founder of the Mahanubhav sect, visited the caves in 1268 and lived here for ten months. According to him, the caves were carved by one Kokasa, a carpenter. This story is also given in the *Katha-kalpataru*. Ellora was thus known and was not lost as was the case with Ajanta. But that is why several sculptures were disfigured in the seventeenth century by Muslim invaders when Aurangzeb was the Mughal viceroy of the Deccan at Aurangabad.

The sacred character of Ellora was probably due to the location of one of the *Jyotir-lingas* (phallus in the form of fire), which has been referred to as Ghrishneshvar. The present temple of Ghrishneshvara in the village was built by Ahilyadevi (1725–95), a Holkar princess of Indore state in Central India. The references to it in the early literature are of a much earlier period and it is therefore highly likely that the Kailas cave was the original *jyotir-linga*. Its name may have been derived from the fact that it is rock-cut. In Sanskrit, *ghrish* means to chisel; hence *Ghrishneshvara*, meaning the god whose shrine is chiselled out.

A few foreigners visited Ellora in the mediaeval period. The earliest was Al-Masudi (tenth century AD) and later Ferishta (ca. 1560–1620), followed by European travellers in the eighteenth and nineteenth century. They include Thevenot, Anquetil du Peron (1758), Sir Charles Malet (1794), Colonel Seely and many others. The caves were formerly protected by the Nizam's government as they were in the old Hyderabad state. Presently they are under the charge of Archaeological Survey of India, New Delhi, and are a world heritage monument.

Photography is allowed but for special filming permission of the Director General, Archaeological Survey of India, Janpath, New Delhi 110011, has to be obtained.

THREE

Site Development at Ellora

Rock-cutting activity at Ellora began in the middle of the sixth century, when work at nearby Ajanta was almost complete. The Hindus were the first to excavate caves at Ellora. It was probably during the reign of the Kalachuris that work began at Ellora Caves 28, 27 and 19, which are modest excavations without any artistic pretensions. Next, work began at what is now Cave 29 (Dumar *lena*), a very ambitious project that resembles the main cave at Elephanta in plan and other essential details, especially the sculptures. Almost simultaneously, Caves 20 and 26 were also excavated. But far more exquisite and aesthetically superior is Cave 21 (Rameshwar) which was also taken up at that time.

It was towards the close of the sixth century, that the excavation of the Buddhist caves at Ellora began. Although it is generally presumed that the Buddhist caves were the first to be excavated, close analytical studies have revealed that rock-cutting activity began in the Hindu caves in the middle of the sixth century, and by the seventh century, work was underway both in the Hindu and the Buddhist caves. The Buddhist activity, however, came to an end by the close of the seventh century and the eighth century is marked by vigorous Hindu activity in the area. Their grandest edifice at Ellora is Cave 16 (Kailas) which can be assigned to the latter half of the eighth century. Work on the Jaina caves started towards the close of the eighth century and continued in full swing in the ninth and tenth centuries. Ellora was thus buzzing with art activity for nearly four centuries (ca 550–950).

Some of the surviving Buddhist caves at Ellora are adorned with sculptures, as for instance Caves 10, 11, and 12. The commonest themes are Buddha and the Bodhisattvas. Buddha is generally depicted in three states (*mudras*): meditating (*dhyana mudra*), preaching (*vyakhyana mudra*) and touching the ground with the index finger of his right hand, (*bhumi-sparsha mudra*). In these he is generally flanked by Bodhisattvas; Padmapani holding a lotus flower and Vajrapani holding a thunderbolt (*vajra*). Besides there are devotees, male and female, and Vidyadharas flying above.

The meditating posture represents the severe penance that Buddha performed at Bodhagaya (Bihar) for gaining Enlightenment. After gaining it, he delivered his first sermon to four disciples at Sarnath near Varanasi (UP). The preaching attitude marks this sermon.

Buddha had a cousin, Mara, a villainish character who always created obstacles to prevent Buddha from gaining Enlightenment. Once he even deputed his six beautiful daughters to Buddha to lure him so that he gave up his penance. The day Buddha was to gain Enlightenment, Mara sent his army and demanded that Buddha surrender his place as he himself owned it. Buddha then calls the earth to witness by touching it with his right hand. This event is represented in the panels showing Buddha in the bhumi-sparsha mudra.

Buddha is generally shown seated on a *simhasana* (lion seat) wearing only a robe (*sanghati*). He possesses the marks of great men (*maha-purusha lakshanas*) such as webbed fingers, an *urna* (protrusion between the eyebrows) and *ushnisha* (protrusion on the head). He does not wear any ornaments, though his attendant Buddhisttavas and goddesses wear rich jewellery.

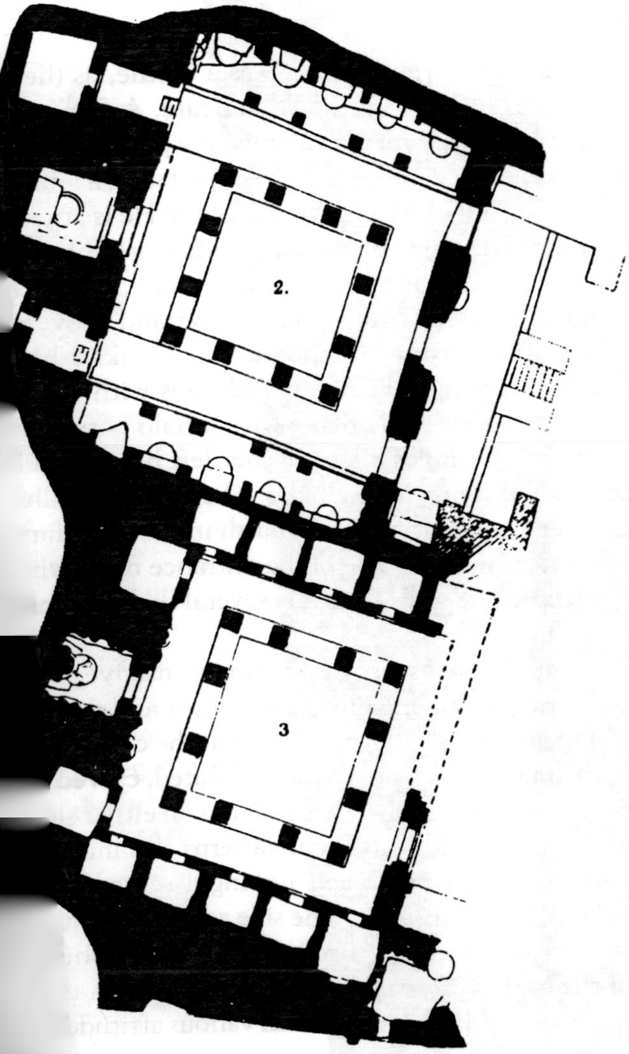

s of Caves 2 and 3.

dra meaning turning the Wheel of Law). He has a e back and is flanked by fly whisk bearers and flying n the side wall is a huge standing Buddha and in the worshippers.

FOUR

Buddhist Caves

Buddhism

Buddha, the founder of Buddhism, was born in the royal family of the Shakyas at Lumbini, which is now in the Nepalese Terai near the Indian border. It is said that his mother Mahamaya, when pregnant, saw in a dream a white elephant holding a lotus entering her body. The royal astrologer interpreted this as symbolic of her having conceived a son who would be a universal emperor or teacher. Buddha was born in 566 BC (or 624 BC according to the Nepalese tradition), was named Siddharth and his *gotra* (family name) was Gautama. He was married to Yashodhara, but he was never interested in the material world. His father did try to divert his attention by holding dance shows and music concerts for him, but in vain.

Four particular events that he witnessed changed his life. An old man suffering from infirmities, a very sick man, and a dead body. But then one day he saw a beggar who was at peace with himself and enjoyed inward joy. He was convinced that he must strive for relieving human beings from suffering. He therefore renounced his kingdom and became a wandering ascetic.

He gained Enlightenment while meditating under a Bodhi (*Ficus religiosa*) tree at Gaya in Bihar. He then began preaching and taught people how to reduce their suffering. Soon he got many followers, including members of the royalty. He died (*maha-nirvana*) at the age of 80 in 486 BC at Kapilavastu, presently called Piprahwa in Uttar Pradesh.

Buddhism soon spread almost all over India, save the deep south. The earlier worship was symbolic; the Bodhi tree, the empty throne, Buddha's foot prints, *triratna* (literally meaning three jewels; Buddha, *dharma* (religion) and *samgha* (monastic order), were the objects of veneration. It was in the first century AD that there was a schism and a new sect known as the Mahayanists introduced the worship of the Buddha image. In the early centuries of the Christian era, Buddhism spread outside India in Central Asia, South Asia and even the Far East but in India itself, the land of its origin, it began to decline from the sixth–seventh centuries onwards. Later it was confined to eastern India only and after the Muslim invasions in the thirteenth century, it disappeared from the country.

It was formerly thought that the Buddhist caves at Ellora were the first to be excavated at the site, with caves 1 to 5 in the first phase (450–600 AD) and 6 to 12 in the later phase (mid seventh—mid eighth century AD). But it is now clear that some of the Hindu Caves (27, 29, 21, 28, 19, 26, 20, 17 and 14) precede the Buddhist. In the Buddhist group, Cave 6 is the earliest, followed by 5, 2, 3, 5 (right wing), 4, 7, 8, 10, 9, and 11 and 12 were the last. They all belong to ca. 630–700 AD. In this book, the caves have been described in the numerical order from 1 to 34.

It is convenient to start with cave 1 as it is close to the road from Aurangabad.

Cave 1

It is in ruins and does not contain anything of note. It is a vihara with eight cells, four in the back wall and four in the right wall. It once had a verandah in the front with a cell.

Cave 2

This is a large cave **[Fig. 4.1]**. It was
Buddha panels in side walls would ind
to a verandah at the north end of which
wearing jewellery, a jewelled headdress
hand and a bag full of coins in the left
whisk bearer. This is Jambhala, the Bu
once was a similar figure at the south
attendant and a flying figure holding

The entrance door of the ca
(*dvarapalas*) wearing elaborate hea
valaya). There is a female figure w
the door, and she holds a lotus in
attendants and flying Vidyadharas
Tara. Over the head of the gu
Vidyadharas. On either side of th
been pierced in the wall. There are
wall as well.

The square hall is supported b
on a platform and having high sc
Some of them have small dwarf fi
shafts; their upper parts are roun
arabesque patterns. The hall has
of which are adorned with flor
back are compartments, each
flanked by fly whisk bearers. Th
excavated later. Some of the
end of the back wall is a doub
There are several Buddha figu
wall.

The shrine in the back w
On the left is Padmapani h
Amitabha in his headdress.
headdress can be seen a stup
worshipper each. The shrine c
on a lion throne; he is shown i

Fig. 4.1. Pla

pravartana mu
huge halo at t
Vidyadharas. (
corner are fou

FOUR

Buddhist Caves

Buddhism

Buddha, the founder of Buddhism, was born in the royal family of the Shakyas at Lumbini, which is now in the Nepalese Terai near the Indian border. It is said that his mother Mahamaya, when pregnant, saw in a dream a white elephant holding a lotus entering her body. The royal astrologer interpreted this as symbolic of her having conceived a son who would be a universal emperor or teacher. Buddha was born in 566 BC (or 624 BC according to the Nepalese tradition), was named Siddharth and his *gotra* (family name) was Gautama. He was married to Yashodhara, but he was never interested in the material world. His father did try to divert his attention by holding dance shows and music concerts for him, but in vain.

Four particular events that he witnessed changed his life. An old man suffering from infirmities, a very sick man, and a dead body. But then one day he saw a beggar who was at peace with himself and enjoyed inward joy. He was convinced that he must strive for relieving human beings from suffering. He therefore renounced his kingdom and became a wandering ascetic.

He gained Enlightenment while meditating under a Bodhi (*Ficus religiosa*) tree at Gaya in Bihar. He then began preaching and taught people how to reduce their suffering. Soon he got many followers, including members of the royalty. He died (*maha-nirvana*) at the age of 80 in 486 BC at Kapilavastu, presently called Piprahwa in Uttar Pradesh.

Buddhism soon spread almost all over India, save the deep south. The earlier worship was symbolic; the Bodhi tree, the empty throne, Buddha's foot prints, *triratna* (literally meaning three jewels; Buddha, *dharma* (religion) and *samgha* (monastic order), were the objects of veneration. It was in the first century AD that there was a schism and a new sect known as the Mahayanists introduced the worship of the Buddha image. In the early centuries of the Christian era, Buddhism spread outside India in Central Asia, South Asia and even the Far East but in India itself, the land of its origin, it began to decline from the sixth–seventh centuries onwards. Later it was confined to eastern India only and after the Muslim invasions in the thirteenth century, it disappeared from the country.

It was formerly thought that the Buddhist caves at Ellora were the first to be excavated at the site, with caves 1 to 5 in the first phase (450–600 AD) and 6 to 12 in the later phase (mid seventh—mid eighth century AD). But it is now clear that some of the Hindu Caves (27, 29, 21, 28, 19, 26, 20, 17 and 14) precede the Buddhist. In the Buddhist group, Cave 6 is the earliest, followed by 5, 2, 3, 5 (right wing), 4, 7, 8, 10, 9, and 11 and 12 were the last. They all belong to ca. 630–700 AD. In this book, the caves have been described in the numerical order from 1 to 34.

It is convenient to start with cave 1 as it is close to the road from Aurangabad.

Cave 1

It is in ruins and does not contain anything of note. It is a vihara with eight cells, four in the back wall and four in the right wall. It once had a verandah in the front with a cell.

Cave 2

This is a large cave **[Fig. 4.1]**. It was a shrine, as the number of Buddha panels in side walls would indicate. A flight of step leads to a verandah at the north end of which is a pot bellied seated figure wearing jewellery, a jewelled headdress (*mukuta*), a lotus in his right hand and a bag full of coins in the left hand. He is attended by a fly whisk bearer. This is Jambhala, the Buddhist god of wealth. There once was a similar figure at the southern end, of which only the attendant and a flying figure holding a garland above remain.

The entrance door of the cave is flanked by guardians (*dvarapalas*) wearing elaborate headdresses with haloes (*prabhuvalaya*). There is a female figure with a halo between them and the door, and she holds a lotus in her left hand, and has female attendants and flying Vidyadharas. She is the Buddhist goddess Tara. Over the head of the guardians are garland-bearing Vidyadharas. On either side of the entrance door, windows have been pierced in the wall. There are several Buddhas carved on this wall as well.

The square hall is supported by twelve massive pillars standing on a platform and having high square bases and cushion capitals. Some of them have small dwarf figures at the corners of the square shafts; their upper parts are round and fluted, carved with elegant arabesque patterns. The hall has galleries on either side, the fronts of which are adorned with floral patterns and musicians. At the back are compartments, each having a seated Buddha figure flanked by fly whisk bearers. The side galleries seem to have been excavated later. Some of the figures are unfinished. On either end of the back wall is a double cell in line with the side aisles. There are several Buddha figures in various attitudes on the front wall.

The shrine in the back wall is flanked by huge Boddhisattvas. On the left is Padmapani holding a lotus stalk with a figure of Amitabha in his headdress. On the right is Vajrapani, in whose headdress can be seen a stupa. They are both attended by a female worshipper each. The shrine contains a colossal Buddha image seated on a lion throne; he is shown in the preaching attitude (*dharmachakra-*

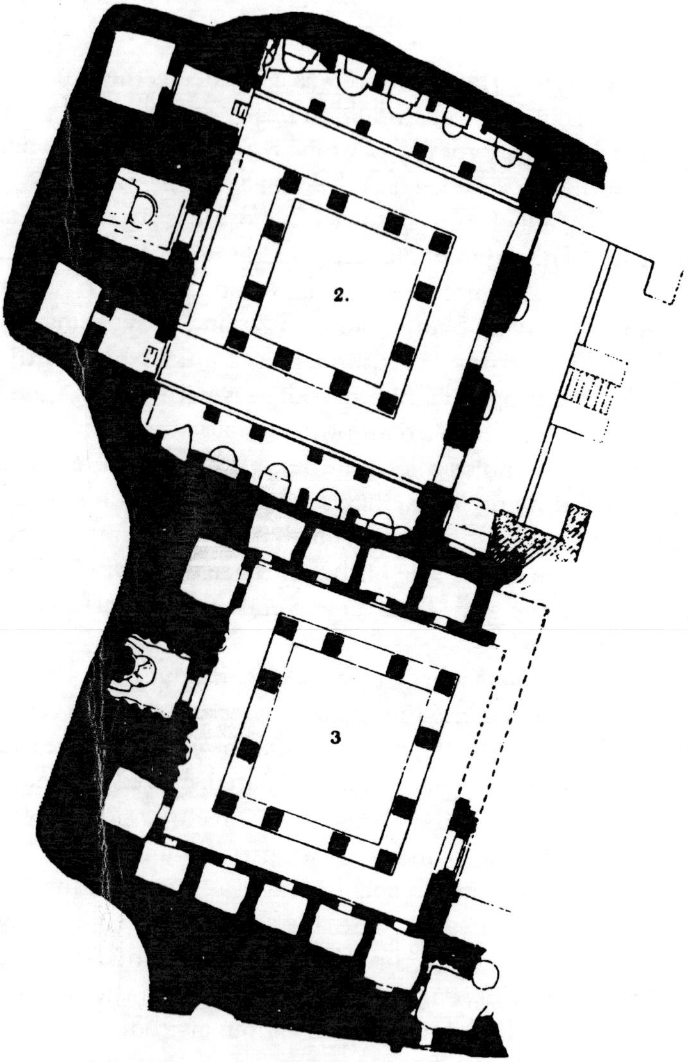

Fig. 4.1. Plans of Caves 2 and 3.

pravartana mudra meaning turning the Wheel of Law). He has a huge halo at the back and is flanked by fly whisk bearers and flying Vidyadharas. On the side wall is a huge standing Buddha and in the corner are four worshippers.

Cave 3

The plan of this cave is similar to that of Cave 2 except that there are cells in the side walls instead of sculptured panels **[Fig 4.1]**. This was clearly a vihara where monks used to live. The structure is incomplete. Situated at a slightly lower level, it is squarish on plan and is supported by twelve pillars with square shafts. There are twelve cells, five each in the side walls and two in the back wall on either side of the central shrine. There were cells in the central verandah as well, one each on either side but the one on the right is completely ruined. On the left wall is an unfinished carved Buddha with attendants.

There is a small chapel in the left side of the verandah which contains a Buddha seated in the cross-legged posture on a lotus seat (padmasana). He is shown touching the ground with his right hand (bhumi-sparsha mudra). He is seated on a lotus, the stalk of which is supported by cobra kings (*naga-rajas*) with hoods over their heads. The god is flanked by fly whisk bearers while Vidyadharas are seen hovering above.

To the right of this panel is Bodhisattva's litany. In the Buddhist pantheon, Bodhisattvas are divinities who have not yet reached the state of the Buddha. The litany of Bodhisattva Avalokiteshvara depicts the god standing, with four panels on either side, each depicting devotees in danger, are praying to god to save them. Merchants and traders were attracted towards Buddhism. They used to transport goods and materials over long distances. Their journey was fraught with hazards and perils. Hence they worshipped the Bodhisattvas for safe travel. These eight great dangers are depicted in the panel: on the left are fire, dacoits, chains, and a shipwreck and on the right are a lion, a cobra, an elephant, and death. In the centre stands Avalokiteshvara, protecting his devotees from the 'eight great dangers' (*ashta-maha-bhayas*).

Cave 4

This double storied cave is smaller than Cave 3 but is considerably ruined. The front is completely damaged and the cells in the squarish hall are unfinished. On the left is the image of a seated Padmapani. There is a small image of Buddha in his crown. He holds a rosary in his right hand, and a lotus in his left and wears deer skin (*ajina*) on his left shoulder. He is flanked by female attendants. The one on his right holds a lotus bud in her right hand while the other, on his left, holds a rosary in her right hand. Above, on the left, is carved a standing Buddha and on the right is a seated Buddha with his right hand raised in the manner of granting protection (abhaya-mudra). Two pillars separate the vestibule from the hall. In the back wall is a shrine in the centre, with a guardian on either side. Inside is a seated Buddha shown in teaching attitude (vyakhyana mudra). There are tall attendants and female fly whisk bearers wearing jewellery. To the west of the cell door is Padmapani. On either end of the back wall is a cell.

In this cave also, there is a litany of Avalokiteshvara in a small shrine, but it is considerably ruined. On the left are four small compartments depicting devotees praying to the god to protect them from assault, a man with a sword, imprisonment, and shipwreck.

Cave 4 (upper)

There is no passage to this cave, which is situated above Cave 4 and to the north of Cave 3, and is connected with Cave 5 on the south side; it is in a very dilapidated state. What remains is a shrine containing a Buddha with attendants. It has a circumbulatory passage. There is a female holding a lotus stalk and may therefore be identified as the Buddhist goddess Tara. A few cells have also survived.

Cave 5

This cave is locally known as Maharwada, indicating that it may have been occupied for some time in the medieval period by people belonging to the Mahar caste, a backward community in Maharashtra. It is a large vihara with cells in side walls and is unique because of its peculiar plan **[Fig. 4.2]**. The front portion has now entirely disappeared, possibly because of landslides. The large hall is supported by 24 massive pillars with squarish shafts and cushion capitals. The

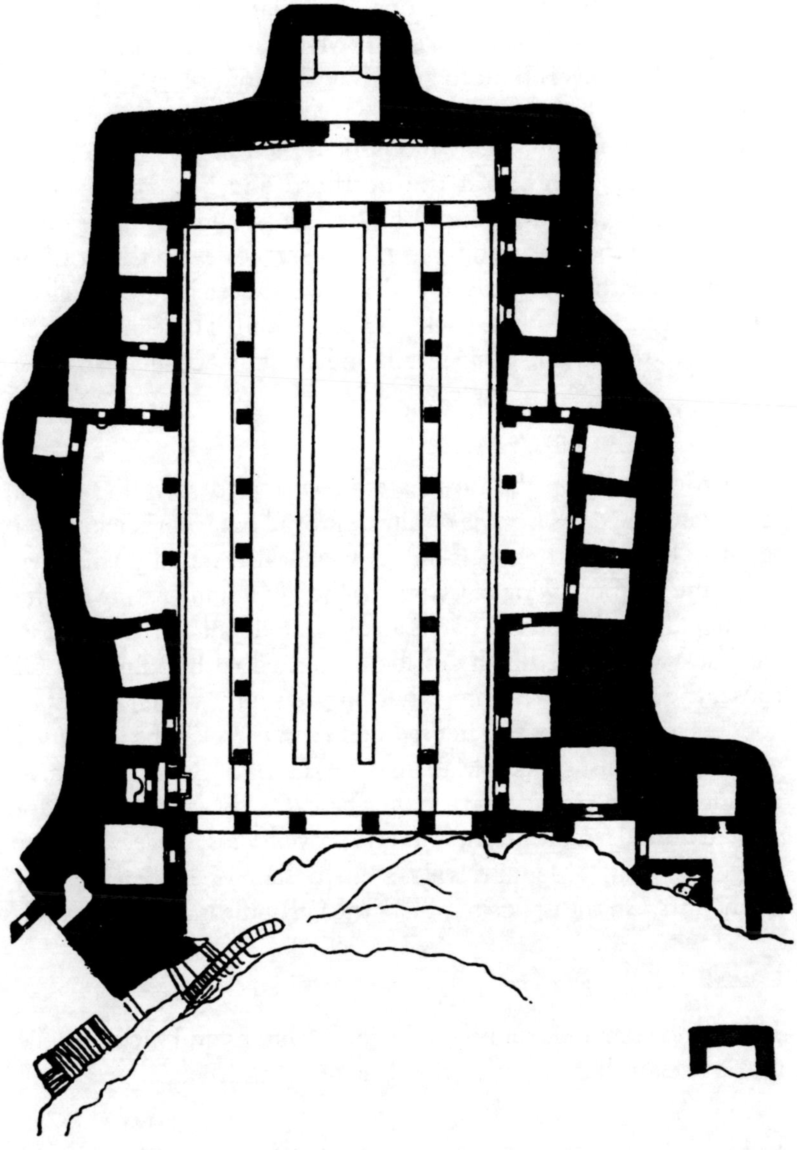

Fig. 4.2. Plan of Cave 5.

space in between is divided into three aisles or bays by two raised rock-cut platforms reminding one of similar arrangement in the Darbar cave at Kanheri in the city of Mumbai. The exact function of these platforms is hard to guess but it is not unlikely that they were meant for keeping religious texts for monks, or the cave may have been a refectory where monks had their meals.

Near the entrance at the northern end is a small shrine containing a seated Buddha with attendants, and on each side of the entrance too are attendants in arched recesses. In the north is Padmapani with two female attendants, wearing elaborate jewellery. The main shrine is in the back wall of the hall. There are pillared recesses in the middle of side walls and a number of squarish cells.

Cave 6

Next to Cave 5, on the north are a few steps descending into a dilapidated cave. Its front is totally destroyed but what remains is a squarish hall with three cells in the back wall. Actually, this cave forms the southern wing of Cave 6 as there is a similar wing on the north and in between the two is an elongated hall with a shrine in the back wall, joined by a vestibule adorned with sculptures. Of these, the most interesting is that on the south, which depicts a goddess with a peacock to her right and can therefore be identified with the Buddhist goddess Mahamayuri. **[Fig. 4.3]**. Nearby is a male reading a manuscript kept on a folding table. On the left is Padmapani with male and female attendants and vidyadharas above. Another image, probably of Manjusri is also seen. In the shrine is Buddha with attendants. On the opposite wall of the vestibule is a similar panel.

Cave 7

This ruined vihara is supported by four columns and has five cells in the back wall; those on either side are unfinished.

Cave 8

This cave can be entered from Cave 7 through a roughly cut passage, which was probably originally intended as a cell in the north wall but

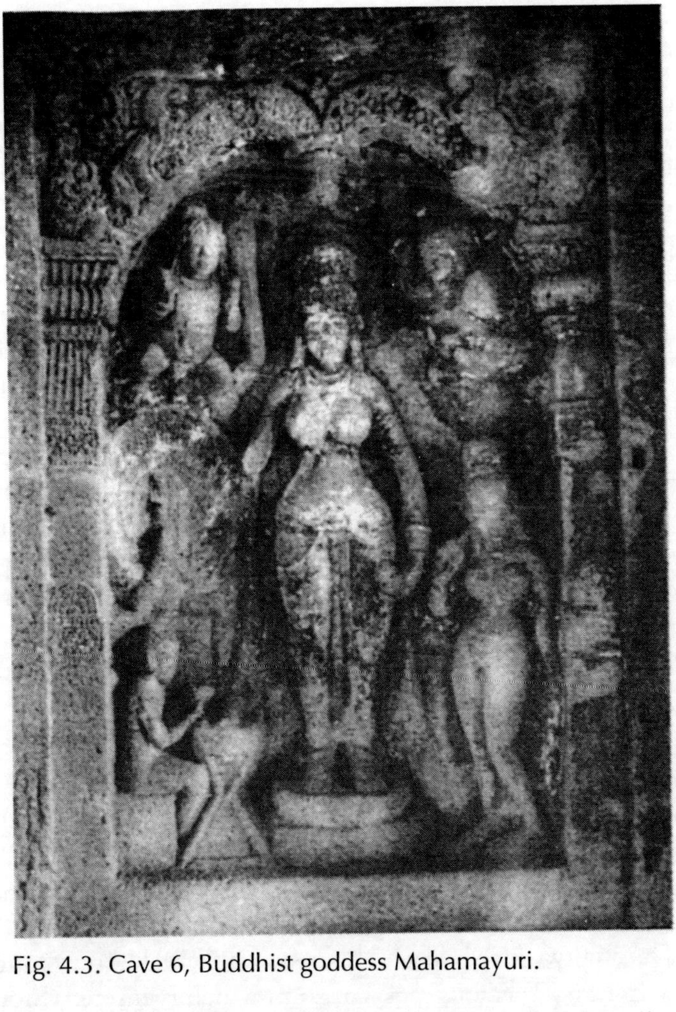

Fig. 4.3. Cave 6, Buddhist goddess Mahamayuri.

remained unfinished. The hall has three cells in the left wall, and a pillared vestibule separates it from the shrine in the back wall, which has a seated Buddha with attendants—one of whom is Padmapani. There are also a number of Vidyadharas. The shrine has a circumambulatory passage. At the southern entrance of this passage is carved an image of Mahamayuri, similar to that in Cave 6. On the north is a chapel with Buddha flanked by attendants, and Vajrapani with a female attendant. The cave resembles Cave 14 (*Ravan ki-khai*) in its plan and can therefore be assigned to ca. 700 AD.

Cave 9

This cave is in a ruined condition and what remains is a sculptured group over the facade, which is interesting. It is carved with small bands depicting Buddha and Bodhisattvas above which are chaitya windows containing Buddha figures. But more interesting is the litany of Tara. Tara is the Buddhist goddess of navigation and was worshipped by traders, particularly those engaged in overseas trade. This was the period (sixth–seventh centuries AD) when Indians had started migrating to South-east Asia for trade and therefore Tara became a very important deity in the Buddhist pantheon. In the panel are shown a snake, a sword, and an elephant on her left and a fire and a shipwreck on her right. This is the only litany of Tara in western India. On the back wall of the cave are carved three panels separated by pilasters with cushion capitals. In the central panel, Buddha is shown seated in the European fashion (pralamba-pada-asana) and in a preaching attitude with Padmapani on his left, and probably Vajrapani on his right with attendants and flying Vidyadharas.

Cave 10

Locally known as 'Vishvakarma' or '*Sutar-ka-jhopda*' (meaning 'carpenter's hut'), this cave is the finest of the Buddhist group at Ellora. It is the only *chaitya-griha* (a prayer hall) in the Buddhist group and it follows the Ajanta pattern of Caves 19 and 26, and is also adorned with exquisite sculptures as at Ajanta **[Fig. 4.4]**.

The chaitya once had a high screen wall which is now ruined. At the front is a spacious rock-cut court which is entered through a flight of steps. On either side are pillared verandahs with chambers in their back walls, which may have been included as subsidiary shrines but are unfinished. The pillared verandah of the chaitya has a small shrine at either end and a single cell in the far end of the back wall. The corridor pillars have massive squarish shafts and vase-and-foliage (*ghata-pallava*) capitals. This type of capital is characteristic of the Gupta period, which is referred to as 'The Golden Age' in Indian history. The vase (*ghata*) filled with foliage (*pallava*) is a symbol of prosperity in Hindu mythology.

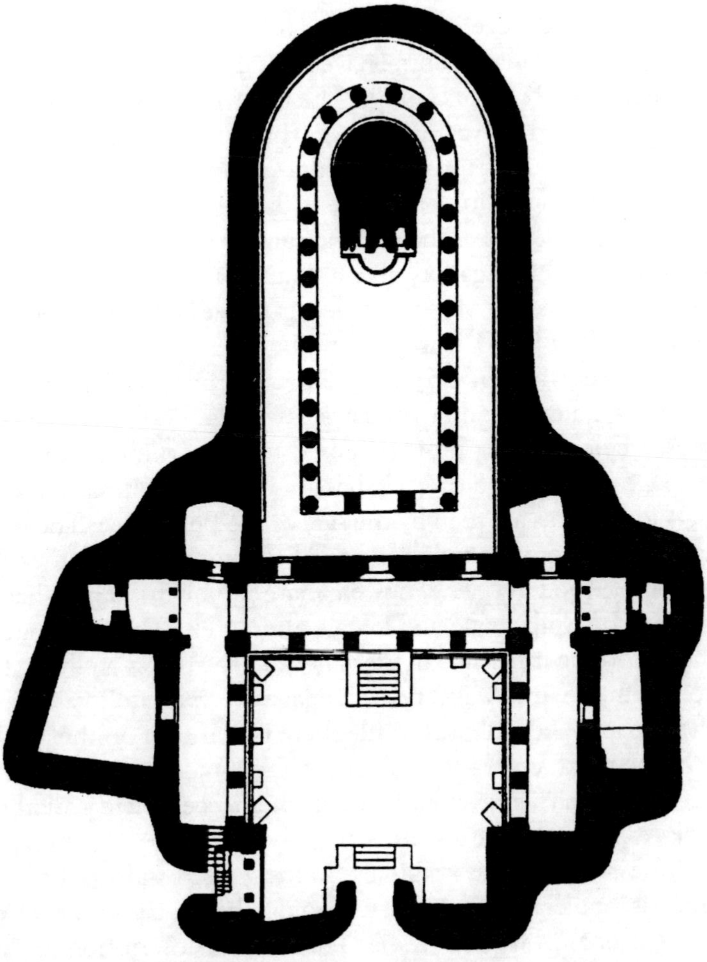

Fig. 4.4. Plan of Cave 10.

The facade of the cave is quite impressive. From the front it becomes clear that the temple has an upper storey over the entrance, which was probably the musicians' gallery. It has a pillared verandah crowned by a fully developed trefoil arch flanked by a Vidyadhara with attendants. On the parapet of the gallery are carved human couples in the upper band and elephants in the lower, on the projecting edge.

The main hall is very spacious and is quite high. It is apsidal on plan and is divided into a central nave and side aisles by 28 octagonal pillars with plain bracket capitals. The triforium over the pillars of the nave is divided into compartments that contain Buddha figures in the dharma-chakra-pravartana mudra (turning the wheel of law), i.e. in a preaching attitude; and he is flanked by attendants and dwarfs below. Inside, near the entrance are two squarish pillars that support the musicians gallery above. In the apsidal end of the hall is a stupa on the face of which is carved, in a recessed arch, a colossal Buddha (3.30 m high) seated in the European fashion with his feet hanging down **[Fig. 4.5]**. He is shown in the teaching attitude (vyakhyana mudra) and at the back is a huge Bodhi tree (Ficus religiosa) below which he is supposed to have gained universal knowledge while meditating. He has attendants on either side and flying Vidyadharas are seen by the side of the Bodhi tree. The hall has a vaulted roof in which ribs have been carved in the rock in imitation of wooden ones. They emanate from behind *naga* busts carved on the walls, male and female alternately. There are more sculptures on the inner side of the gallery. In the recess on the right side of the front window is carved an image of Avalokiteshvara with attendants and Vidyadharas, while there is Manjusri on the north side. In the north end of the balcony is Tara holding a lotus above which are Buddha figures while in the southern recess there is another Avalokiteshvara with attendants.

In the court there is a staircase in the western side at the end of which is a gallery. This cave can be said to be the last of the rock-cut *chaityagrihas* in western India. There is one inscription in the cave that is engraved in the balcony. It is the usual Buddhist formula:

Ye dharma hetu prabhava hetum,
tesam Tathagato hyavadattesam cha
yo nirodha evam vadi maha-sramana

'All things proceed from cause; this cause has been declared by Tathagata (Buddha); all things will cease to exist; that is, that which is declared by the great sramana (Buddha).'

On stylistic grounds, the cave can be assigned to ca 700 AD.

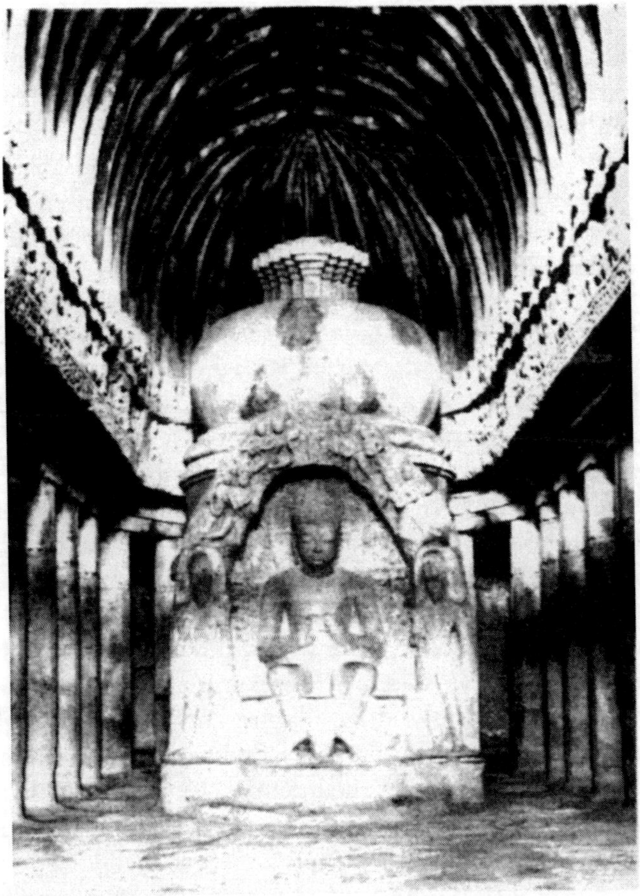

Fig. 4.5. Cave 10 (Vishvakarma), interior of the chaitya with Buddha image carved over the stupa.

Cave 11

Just to north of Cave 10 is Cave 11, which is locally known as Do Thal, meaning double storied, but is actually three storied as the excavation carried out in 1876–7 revealed its ground floor. It has a spacious rock-cut court in front. To the left of the entrance is a shrine of Avalokiteshvara, which can be approached by a flight of steps. The main deity is identified as Rakta Lokeshvara who is shown seated cross-legged with Tara on his right and a four-armed Bhrikuti on his left. Yet another goddess, Chunda, who is seen on the left wall, is also four armed. On the right wall is Buddha whose head is broken; he is flanked by Bodhisattvas. The Hindu deities Durga and Ganesha, which are also seen in the right court, are later additions.

The ground floor has a long pillared verandah with a shrine in the middle of the back wall containing a Buddha figure flanked by Padmapani and Vajrapani. On the left is yet another cell and in the left hand corner is a staircase that goes to the upper (first) floor.

The first floor has a long pillared verandah with three shrines in the back wall. The first on the left is an unfinished cell and the next is a small shrine containing a huge seated image of Buddha. In front of him is a female devotee on the floor holding a jar, she is probably Sujata affering food to Buddha. There is yet another devotee prostrating before him. Buddha himself is shown in the bhumi-sparsha-mudra in which he is calling the earth for witness. He is flanked by Padmapani on his right and Vajrapani on his left, whose thunderbolt is seen on the lotus. On the side walls of the shrine are the figures of the Bodhisattvas, of which three can be identified with certainty: Maitreya holding a flower and a miniature stupa in his crown; Sthirachakra holding a sword and Jnanaketu with a pennan. Above them on both side are Buddha figures. Jambhala, the Buddhist lord of wealth—the counterpart of Kubera in the Hindu pantheon—is carved on the left of the entrance. Below him is a man with a pot of coins and on the right is Tara holding a lotus.

The central shrine is joined to the verandah by a large hall with two pillars. In the shrine is a collossal Buddha seated in the bhumi-sparsha mudra (touching the ground with his right hand); he is flanked by Padmapani and Vajrapani. The next shrine in the back wall also has a seated image of Buddha with the usual paraphernalia. Next to this is a small cell with a rock-cut bench but more interesting is a small shrine carved in the right (south) end of the verandah containing a seated Buddha with attendants; there are three standing female figures on the left and three male figures on the right, who may be Bodhisattvas.

At the left end of the verandah is a staircase which leads to the top floor, which again consists of a pillared verandah and a shrine in the centre of the back wall similar to that on the first floor. There is another shrine in the northeastern corner containing an image of Buddha with his attendants. Yet another shrine was intended in the southern half but was given up. On the walls are many small figures of Buddha, and Padmapani with four hands, besides a female, holding lotus buds. In the rock-cut court on the ground floor are several cells. One of them contains a headless Buddha, a seated Lokeshvar and other sculptures. The Hindu deities Mahisha-mardini Durga and Ganesha, which are seen on the right wall of the hall, are later additions.

Cave 12

Yet another three-storied cave, like 11, which is known as *Tin Thal*. It has a spacious rock-cut court which can be entered through a flight of steps as it is situated at a slightly higher level. In the north side of the court is a small cave with two pillars and a cistern.

The ground floor consists of a large hall, an oblong vestibule and a shrine. The hall is supported by eight pillars in three rows, the front ones of which have plain squarish shafts and bracket capitals while those in the middle row are carved with floral designs at the top. In a large compartment on the back wall, to the left of the shrine, is a sculpture in nine panels representing the Buddha mandala, the magic diagram of the Cosmos. In the centre is a seated Buddha with fly whisk bearers and to his left and right are Padmapani and Vajrapani. In the upper row is a seated Bodhisattva (Rakta Lokeshvar); the central panel has a Sthirachakra holding a sword in his left hand while the third one is probably Jnanaketu with a flower stalk in his left hand. The first figure in the bottom row is again Jnanaketu holding a pennan; the next in the middle is also a Bodhisattva holding a lotus stalk. The last is probably Manjusri. The images of Bodhisattvas cannot be identified with certainty as their attributes are not clearly seen but they all wear rich jewellery.

In the corresponding position on the northern side was a seated Buddha image which is now destroyed. In the north side are rock cut beds for monks. In the central recess, to the right and left of the vestibule, are Buddha images on lion seats; the left attendants in each case hold lotus flowers.

There are several smaller panels on the pilaster of the third aisle. One of them depicts Vajrasattva flanked by Padmapani and Vajrapani; and below is an image of Tara holding a lotus stalk. There are also Buddha figures with attendants. On the second pilaster, on the left wall of the vestibule, the panel on the left shows Buddha and below this the four-armed Buddhist goddess Chunda. In one of her right hands, she holds a bowl while the other holds a rosary and is in *abhaya mudra* (granting protection). One of the left hands holds a lotus stalk. Next to this is another figure of Chunda holding similar attributes but in one of the left hands is a ladle (*sruk*); she wears a cylindrical headdress.

In the niche on the left in the vestibule is a Buddha with Bodhisattvas, fly whisk bearers flanking him, and Vidyadharas above.

The shrine door has a Maitreya on the right and a Manjusri on the left, both holding flowers but the latter has a book on it. The shrine contains a colossal image of Buddha and on side walls there are five dhyani (meditating) Buddhas. Below them are still larger figures: from the left, the first is Padmapani holding lotus, the second is Jnanaketu with a flag, the third is Sthirachakra with a sword and *triratna*, the fourth holds a flower, while the fifth is mutilated. Above these are seated *dhyani* Buddhas in meditation. On the opposite wall there are four Bodhisattvas whose hands are broken. The third one appears to be Manjusri as there is a book over the lotus in his hand. Above them are five Dhyani Buddhas.

There are 12 cells in the hall of the cave, three each in the side walls and two each flanking the vestibule in the back wall and there are two more in the vestibule on the sides near the front. In the first cell in the south wall is a staircase leading up to the first floor. It leads into a chamber with two pillars and is carved with several sculptures. On the back wall is a Buddha seated on throne and flanked by attendants. Padmapani is seen on the west with a male and female devotee. Besides these there are many smaller figures noteworthy among them being a four armed goddess holding a rosary and a *kamandalu* (water vessel); she may be Bhrikuti.

The stair further leads to the first floor which has a long verandah and a large entrance in the middle having two massive square pillars leading to the hall. There are also entrances near the ends of the verandah. The hall is divided into three aisles by two rows of massive pillars. In each row there are many sculptures on the far end of the vestibule in the centre. They include a Buddha figure, Padmapani with female devotees, and a stupa. Noteworthy among them is the image of a four-armed Bhrikuti on the left wall whereas on the right wall there is Padmapani with Tara on the left and Jambhala on the right.

The shrine door is flanked by guardians. The one on the north is Padmapani, who holds a full blown lotus whereas on the south is Vajrapani with his thunderbolt. Both wear elaborate jewellery and their jewelled belts are very elegant. Inside the shrine is a seated Buddha; in front of whom is a female devotee holding a pot. She is probably Sujata offering food to Buddha. On the other side is yet another attendant standing over a prostrate figure. On either side of the throne are Padmapani and Vajrapani. There are four figures on the side walls while on the front is carved what is probably a donor couple. Above are seven seated Buddhas (Manushi).

In the northern end of the verandah is a staircase that leads to the top floor. There are more figures here, including a seated Buddha; on his seat is carved a wheel (wheel of law-*dharmachakra*) with a deer on either side. There are also attendants and a standing Buddha. In the first landing is seen a horseman with two attendants, above which is a female holding a flower.

The top floor (second floor) of this cave is very impressive as it is completely finished **[Fig. 4.6]**. This is a clear proof that while cutting the caves, work always started from the top and this also shows why the ground floor, which was the last to be carved, has remained unfinished. The top floor consists of a very spacious hall with a vestibule and a shrine in the back wall. The hall is divided into five bays or aisles by five rows of massive squarish pillars, eight in each row and there are two more in the vestibule. On the side walls are recesses at the end of aisles containing large sculptured panels depicting Buddha seated on throne with attendants. At the south end of the back aisle was a panel showing Buddha preaching

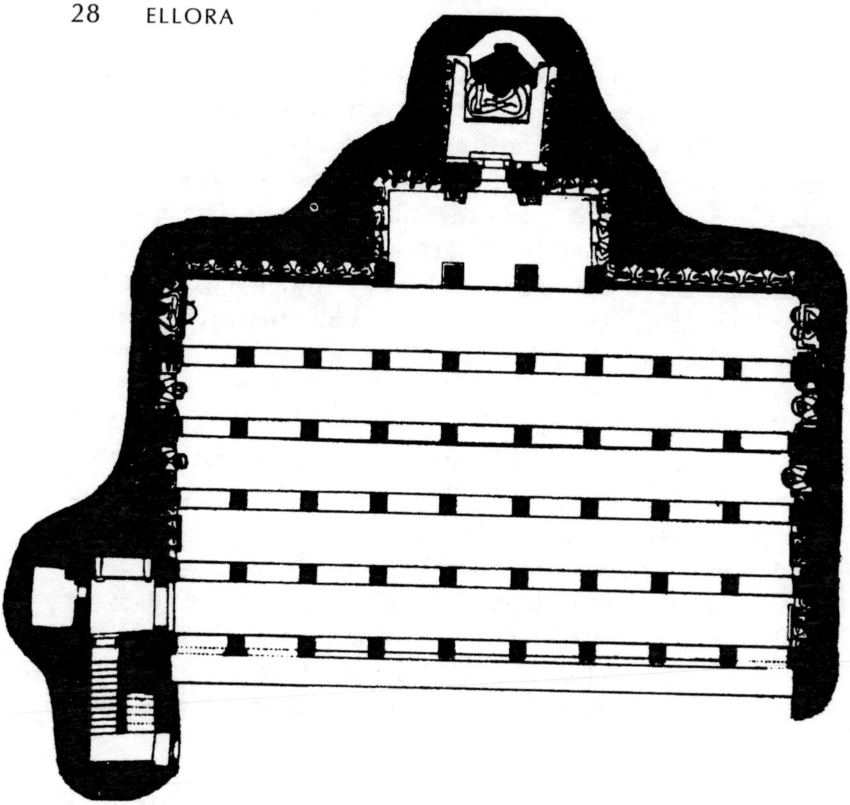

Fig. 4.6. Plan of Cave 12, upper floor.

(*vyakhyana mudra*). On the opposite wall of the same aisle is a panel showing Buddha in a meditating posture (*dhyana mudra*). On either side are panels showing Buddha meditating and preaching Buddha going to heaven to preach his Law to gods and Buddha entering his nirvana (death).

There are more sculptures on the right side of the back wall. On the left are seven *manushi* (human) Buddhas in meditating attitude, each having his distinguishing tree and a halo at his back [**Fig. 4.7**]. It may be recalled that the manushi Buddhas also occur in Ajanta paintings (fifth century AD) in Cave 22, along with their names: Vipashyi, Shikhi, Vishwabhu, Krakuchchhanda, Kanakamuni, Kashyapa and Shakyasimha.

These are the last seven Buddhas whose distinguishing attribute

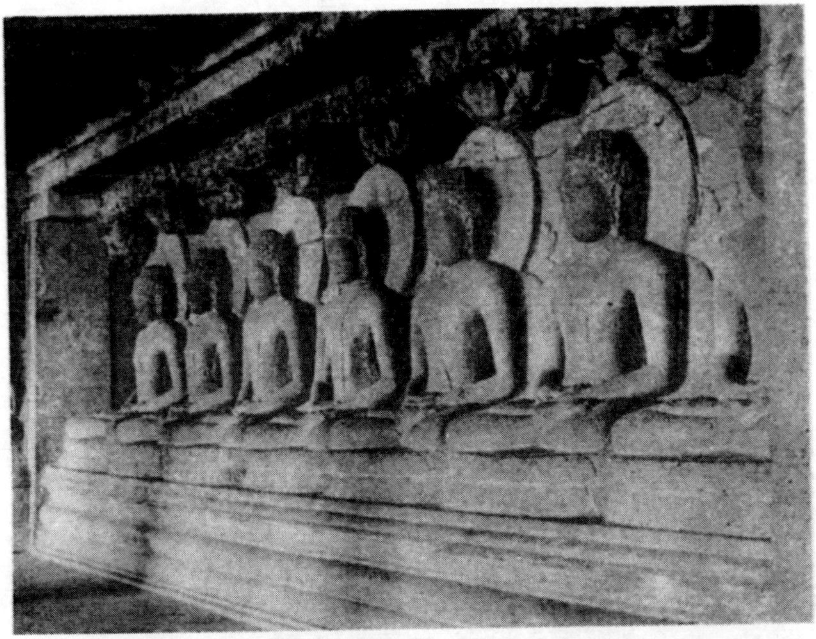

Fig. 4.7. Cave 12, Manushi Buddhas.

is a particular sacred tree, shown at the back of each. According to the Buddhist texts, these are (1) Patali or trumpet flower, (*Bignonia snaveoleus*), (2) *Pundarika*, sweet smelling mango, (3) Shala (*Shorea robusta*) (4) Shirisha (*Acacia sirisa*) (5) Udumbara (*Ficus glomorata*) (6) Nyagrodha (*Ficus indica*), and (7) Pippala (*Ficus religiosa*).

Similarly, on the right side of the back wall there are seven seated Buddha figures shown in the teaching attitude with a nimbus at the back and an umbrella over their heads. They are Bodhisattvas (1) Vairochana, (2) Akshobhya, (3) Ratnasambhava, (4) Amitabha, (5) Amoghasiddhi, (6) Vajrasattva, and (7) Vajraraja.

On the side and back walls of the vestibule are twelve goddesses, three each on the right and left walls as also on the back walls. They are seated on lotuses. The first on the left wall is probably Vajradhatvishvari as she is seen holding a *chintamani* jewel. Next to her is Chunda holding a lotus with a book. Of the three figures on the left side of the back wall, the first is Khadiravani Tara, who is seated on the lotus holding a lotus stalk held by two cobra figures.

The next goddess also holds a lotus stalk, held by cobra by the side of which is a swan. The third figure is also identical. These are the representations of Tara **[Fig. 4.8]**.

On the right side of the back wall is an interesting female figure. Both her waist band and her headdress is made of cobras. She is Janguli. Next is Mahamayuri, if the peacock feather in her left hand is any indication. The third one is holding a water vessel (kamandalu) and she may be Ushanishavijaya. On the right wall of the vestibule, the first is Bhrikuti, the second is Pandara, and the third is Tara.

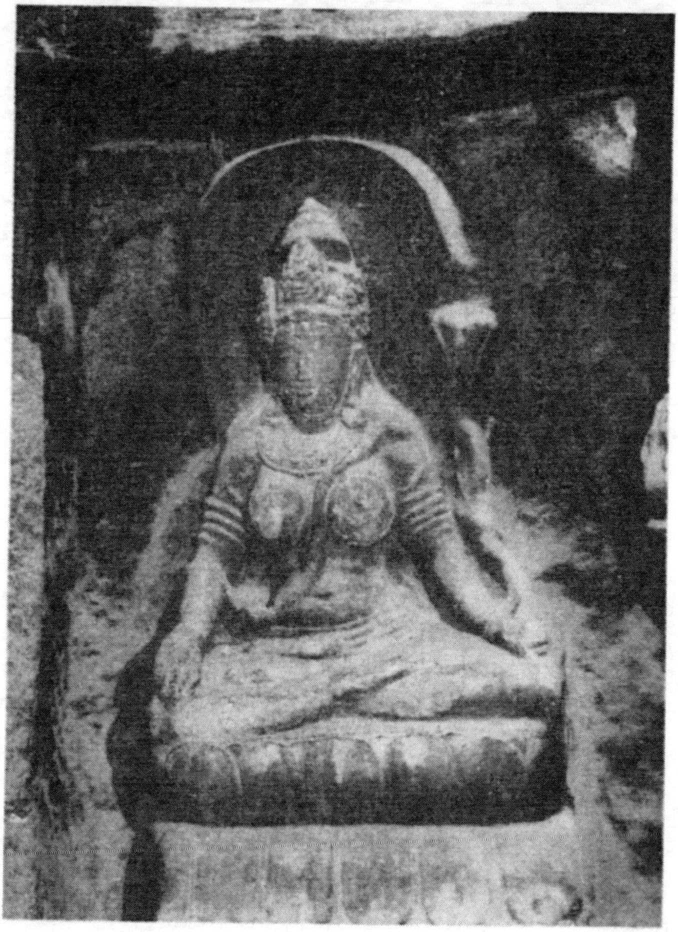

Fig. 4.8. Cave 12, Tin Thal, second floor, Tara in the sanctum.

The shrine contains a seated Buddha image, which was formerly worshipped as a Hindu god. The facial features were obliterated and have been done in plaster probably in the 18th century. On the left is Padmapani and a figure holding a lotus bud; on his right is a male with a sword; one more holds a fly whisk and another may be a devotee. On the right is Vajrapani and four similar figures. On the inner side of the front wall is probably the donor couple, if the male holding the money bag is any indication. Above, on each side, are seated Buddhas.

The cave can be assigned to ca. 700 AD.

Cave 12 is thus one of the most important Buddhist edifices in India. A noteworthy feature of this cave is that it is profusely decorated with sculptures, more particularly of Buddhist goddesses. This is enigmatic in view of the fact that Buddha himself was totally opposed to admission of women in the monastic order, and for a long time there were no nuns in Buddhist establishments as the adherents of the Hinayana faith strictly followed the teaching of the Enlightened One. But with the rise of Mahayana sect from the beginning of the Christian era, first the Buddha and the Bodhisattva images came to be worshipped. Later, women came to be admitted in the Order and in consequence goddesses were also created, first among them being Tara. All this was necessary as Buddhism had to compete with Hinduism, which is characterised by numerous gods and goddesses whose images were worshipped. With the rise of Tantric Shaktism in the fifth and sixth centuries, it did not take too long for its influence to reach the Buddhists. As a result new goddesses appeared in the Buddhist pantheon. The occurrence of so many gods and goddesses in the Buddhist caves at Ellora indicates the emergence of Tantric Buddhism and we may not be far off the mark if we postulate its beginning in western India. It is the dominance of Tantricism which finally led to the decline of Buddhism in India.

FIVE

Hindu Caves

Hinduism

The Hindu pantheon evolved in the historical period from the sixth and fifth centuries BC and developed fully by the fifth and sixth centuries AD, when Hinduism received royal patronage under the Imperial Guptas. This was the period when the Puranas were committed to writing and the two epics—the Mahabharata and the Ramayana,—were given their final form. This was also the period that marks the rise of the Bhakti cult.

Shiva was first worshipped in the human form but came to be represented as a phallus from the beginning of the Christian era. Shiva, Vishnu, and Brahma form the Hindu trinity; with Brahma as the creator, Vishnu as the sustainer, and Shiva as the destroyer. Saivism, Vaishnavism and Shaktism (the cult of goddess) are the three most important cults in Hinduism. A number of divinities came to be associated with them in course of time. Many of them can be seen at Ellora, where numerous panels illustrate Puranic legends and scenes from the epics.

Hindu Caves

Situated in the middle of the complex are the Hindu caves that constitute the largest group (sixteen caves) at Ellora. Work first began on Caves 28, 27, and 19, which are rather modest excavations. The most impressive of the early phase are Cave 29 (Dumar *lena*) and 21, which is far more elegant. Along with them, work was underway at 20 and 26 and slightly later at 17, 19, and 28. They were followed by 14 and 15, which are quite impressive, and the activity culminates in Cave 16 (Kailas) which is the greatest achievement of the Indian genius. All this activity was going on from the middle of the sixth century to the end of the eighth century. Hindu caves are rock-cut temples and differ in concept from those of the Buddhists whose religious needs were different.

Cave 14

At a short distance from Tin Thal (Cave 12), the last Buddhist cave, lies an insignificant excavation (Cave 13) which is almost totally destroyed. On its north is a large Cave (14), locally known as *Ravana ki khai* (Ravana's pit). It is a roughly squarish hall, supported by sixteen pillars of which four are at the front. Many of the pillars have been reconstructed. At the back is an oblong shrine with a circumambulatory passage around it.

The pillars are carved with lavish decorative patterns. They have a squarish lower half ornamented with a floral band, above which is a couple in a chaitya window. Over this is a cabled pattern crowned by the vase-and-foliage capital. The surmounting bracket is adorned with the *Kirtimukha* (demon's head) motif flanked by prancing animals. The pilasters too are highly ornamented with human figures at the base, over which is a band of chaitya arches. Above this are human figures surmounted by peacocks in arches. The upper part of the pilaster is fluted and topped by cushion capitals; the brackets too are carved with human and animals figures.

The walls of the cave are almost fully covered with exquisite sculptures and the cave therefore looks like a sculpture gallery. On the north (left) wall, starting from the front, are:

(1) Goddess Durga with her foot over a lion, her mount; she is four armed with a trident (*trishula*) in her upper right hand, the other hands are broken.

(2) Next is Lakshmi, the consort of Vishnu, seated over lotuses in which cobra kings (naga-rajas) are holding water jars. A tortoise is also seen. She has two arms but her attendants have four, one of them is shown holding a conch (*shankha*), an attribute of Vishnu. Elephants are shown bathing the goddess with water jars and she can be therefore identified as Gaja-Lakshmi.

(3) The boar (*Varaha*) incarnation of Vishnu, with his foot on the great serpent (*Shesha*). He holds Prithvi, the goddess of earth, whom he saves from destruction. A snake demon and figures with cobra hoods are also seen supplicating.

(4) In this panel, Vishnu is shown in his abode Vaikuntha with his consorts Sridevi and Bhudevi; there are four attendants holding fly whisks and below is an eagle, the god's mount, and a few male and female figures, some of them playing on musical instruments. Below this panel are six human figures, two male and four female.

(5) In the following panel, Vishnu and Lakshmi are seen seated under an arch with attendants behind. Below are seven dwarfs, some of them holding musical instruments.

The shrine proper, at the back, has guardians (*dvara-palas*) and a number of devotees. On the left, near the legs of the guardians, is a male dwarf (*gana*) holding a crooked staff while on the other side is a female dwarf (*vamanika*). Besides, there is Ganga on a crocodile on the right and Yamuna on a tortoise on the left. They wear elaborate jewellery and the folds of their garments are very realistically depicted. Inside, near the back wall, is an altar and a broken image of Durga to whom probably the shrine was probably dedicated. In the hall floor are holes that may have been fire pits.

In the southeast corner of the circumambulatory passage is a carved Virabhadra holding a battle axe (*parashu*) and a small hourglass-shaped drum (*damaru*). On his seat is carved a bull, his mount. On the north side are seven mother goddesses, Ganesha and Kala (god of death) and Kali (his consort). Next is Ganesha who is seen eating, with his trunk, sweets from a bowl in his left hand. Beyond him are seven seated mother goddessess (*Sapta-matrikas*), with a halo at the back of each. They all wear lavish jewellery and their tall headresses are noteworthy. The goddesses can be identified from their mounts, which are carved on their pedestals: (1) Chamunda (owl), (2) Indrani (elephant), (3) Varahi (boar), (4) Vaishnavi (eagle), (5) Kaumari (peacock), (6) Maheshwari (bull), and (7) Brahmi (swan).

The next panel on the south wall of the hall depicts the *Andhakasura vadha murti* form of Shiva, as is clear from the stretched hide over his head. Shiva has eight hands, of which the right one holds Andhakasura and the four are stretching the elephant skin over his head. When Shiva wanted to annihilate Andhaka demon, the latter's friend Gajasura, in the form of elephant, attacked Shiva, who then slayed him first. Parvati, Shiva's consort, and his son Ganesha, and a dwarf, are also present.

The next panel depicts the demon king Ravana shaking Mount Kailasa. According to the Puranic story, Ravana, the demon king, was a great devotee of Shiva, but he was also very proud of his prowess, and one day he started shaking Mount Kailasa, the abode of Shiva. Shiva's attendants started running helter-skelter in fear and even his consort Parvati was afraid. Shiva, unmoved, was about to crush Ravana with his toe. Ravana then implored to God to let him go.

In this panel, Ravana is shown with ten heads, shaking the mountain, as a result of which there is chaos everywhere. Shiva is next seen pressing his toe against Ravana. Ravana finally realises Shiva's power and repents. The dwarfs start mocking him.

The third panel on the south wall shows Shiva dancing the Tandava. Three drummers are seen on the left, while Parvati and two more dwarfs are on the right. Behind Shiva is Bhringi, his ardent devotee. There are three musicians with drum flute, and cymbals. Higher up in the sky are other gods; on the left is Indra on an elephant, Agni on a ram and two others, while on the right are Brahma and Vishnu. Shiva in Hindu mythology is known as the master of dance, hence, Nataraja. The dancing Shiva is a very common theme in Indian art, particularly in South India. According to a legend, Shiva went to the Taraka forest to defeat the sages in a philosophical debate. The sages got angry and created a tiger from the sacrificial altar. The tiger pounced on Shiva who, however, killed it and wore its skin. The sages next sent a snake, which Shiva wore as an ornament. Then finally, the sages sent a demon; and Shiva trampled upon him and started dancing. This is the *apasmara purusha* seen under Shiva's feet in Shiva dancing panels.

The next panel depicts Shiva and Parvati playing a game of dice, known as *chausar*. Ganesha, the elephant-headed son of Shiva, and another attendant are seen behind the god. There are two males and a female behind Parvati. Below the bull (*Nandi*), the mount of Shiva and a number dwarfs (ganas) are seen playfully enjoying. Shiva is four armed; his one left hand is shown holding the hand of Parvati, while the other rests on the seat, the remaining two hands are broken.

The first panel depicts Durga killing Mahishasura. She is four armed—two of her hands hold a sword and a trident, while another holds the head of the buffalo demon. The fourth is broken. The demon is also being attacked by Durga's lion.

Mahishasura was the son of Rambha and was born as a gift of Agni, the fire god. He worshipped Brahma and obtained from him a boon by which he would not be killed by any one except a woman. He then became potent with power and started harassing other gods. Therefore Shiva, Vishnu and Brahma created a *maha-shakti* (great female power)—Durga—who ultimately killed him.

Cave 15

This cave is located at a much higher level and one has to climb several steps to reach it. As in Cave 14, this cave too has several sculptures depicting incarnations of divinities and hence is named Dashavatara, which means the 'ten incarnations of Vishnu'. It has a spacious rock-cut court in front, in the centre of which is a rock-cut pavilion (*mandapa*) besides some small shrines and a cistern **[Fig. 5.1]**. The pavilion has a small porch in front supported by two square pillars. There is a perforated window in the west wall over which is engraved a Sanskrit inscription in the Brahmi script of the eighth century. It is, however, incomplete and much of it has been damaged due to weathering. It gives the genealogy of the Rashtrakuta dynasty, from the founder Dantivarman (ca. 600–30) and records the visit of

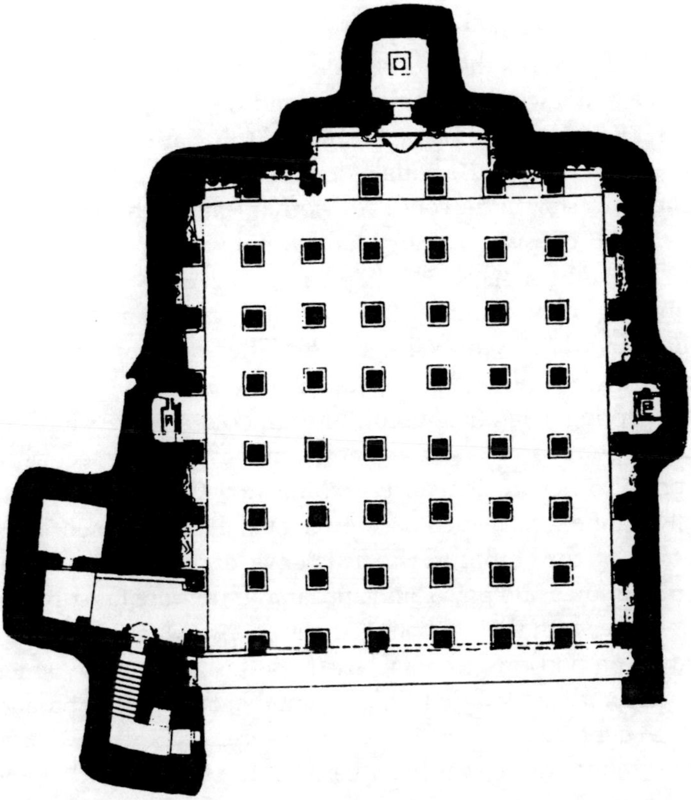

Fig. 5.1. Plan of Cave 15 (Dashavatara), upper floor.

Dantidurga (752–7) to the cave. It can, therefore, be placed in the middle of the eighth century.

The squarish pavilion faces east on a raised platform, which may have served as a pedestal for a Nandi image. The exterior surface of the walls of the pavilion are carved with sculptures and on the flat roof are seen dwarfs and lions at the corners. The entrance has Ganga and Yamuna on the two sides.

This is a double storeyed cave not too different in conception from Caves 11 and 12 of the Buddhist group, which is indicative of their influence on each other. The ground floor is quite spacious, and is supported by 14 square pillars, six each in the first two rows and two in the vestibule. On either side of the vestibule are two cells each. There is a flight of steps in the northern corner of the front aisle and a window on the first landing for light. Here too, sculptures of Ganesha, Surya, Vishnu, Ardhanarishvara, Shiva-Parvati, Durga slaying the buffalo demon and others are carved in low relief. The stair in the southwest corner leads to the upper floor of the cave. It consists of a large hall with a vestibule joining the shrine. The hall is supported by 44 pillars in seven rows of six pillars each, and two on the vestibule. The front pillars are exquisitely carved with floral patterns, snakes and dwarfs. There are corresponding pilasters in side walls and the space in between in the recesses is used for carving magnificent sculptures in bold relief. As in Cave 14, the sculptures on one side are mostly of the Vaishnav sect while those on the other are Shaiva. This shows how the entire cave was carefully planned and meticulously excavated. It must be mentioned that some of the sculptures in this cave are characterised by tremendous force and power and appear as if they are bursting out of their frames with their unbounded raw energy. Many of them are of gigantic proportions, a characteristic of Rashtrakuta art, which reaches its zenith in Cave 16 (Kailasa), another Rashtrakuta product of the 8th century.

The Shaiva *dwarapalas* (guardians) at the front on either end are of huge proportions and are characterised by vigour. The sculptures on the northern side, starting from the front are:

(1) Shiva slaying Andhakasura; he first annihilates the demon in the form of an elephant (Gajasura). The god has stretched the hide of the elephant over his head. Then he kills Andhakasura because he was harassing the Brahmins who were worshipping a *linga* at Varanasi. He is seen thrusting his trident into the demon, while he holds another by one of his left hands. The god wears a garland of skulls (*runda-mala*) and cobra around his neck; his open mouth with projecting teeth add to the horrifying effect. The scene becomes more gruesome by the presence of Kali, whose skeleton is seen holding a curved knife in her right hand and a bowl in the left for collecting the demon's blood. Her symbol, an owl, is seen at the back. In front of her, on the right, is Parvati, the consort of

Shiva. The artist has succeeded in delineating the fierce combativeness of the god.

(2) Shiva dancing with musicians by his side and flying Vidyadharas above; with Parvati and Skanda on the right. The delicate balance displayed by the artist is noteworthy.

(3) There is only a pedestal over which there probably was a Shiva *linga*.

(4) Shiva and Parvati playing the game of dice (*chausar*); Nandi (bull) and the *ganas* (dwarfs) are seen below.

(5) This panel depicts the marriage of Shiva and Parvati (*Kalyana-sundara murti*) with Brahma, the three headed priest below, whereas above gods are seen on their mounts hovering in the sky. A noteworthy change here is that Parvati, the bride, is standing to Shiva's left and not to the right, as is usually shown.

(6) Ravana shaking Kailasa which is aesthetically superior to that in Cave 14.

Of the sculptures on the back wall, the first shows Shiva protecting his devotee, young Markandeya, from the clutches of Yama, the god of death. According to the Puranic story, Markandeya, the son of a sage, was highly intelligent but was fated to die at the age of 14. He was a great devotee of Shiva, so when Yama came to take his life, he clasped a Shiva linga out of which emerged Shiva himself, who drove away Yama. This form of Shiva is known as *Kalari-murti* or Markendeya *anugraha-murti*.

(7) Shiva as *Gangadhara-murti* is seen in the next panel. Parvati is on Shiva's left and Nandi on the right; above is an elephant supporting a sage who is seated on a lotus. Flying Vidhyadharas are seen hovering above. The five human heads near Shiva's feet are those of the sons of Sagara. According to the Puranic story, king Sagara had a son called Asamanjasa who was a wicked person and a bad influence on the other sons as well. The gods therefore complained to Indra. So once, when Sagara was about to perform a horse-sacrifice (*ashva-medha*), Indra captured the horse, took it to the netherworld (*patala*) and hid it in the hermitage of sage Kapila. As Sagara's sons rushed to kill Kapila, the sage reduced them to ashes; they could be brought back to life only by the waters of the Ganga. Bhagirath,

born in Sagara's family, performed severe austerities and brought the Ganga down but the force of the water was such that only Shiva's matted locks (*jata-mukuta*) could hold it. The water was then sprinkled on Sagara's sons and they were brought back to life.

In the vestibule between the hall and the shrine, on the north wall, is a carved Ganesa. On the floor, at the back corners, are lions. To the left of the shrine door on the back wall is seen Parvati on a lotus seat (*padmasana*) with a rosary practising penance for gaining Shiva as her husband. There are musicians on either side. The entrance of the shrine is guarded by four-armed *dwarapalas* (door-keepers) holding a club, a snake, and a thunderbolt. Inside the shrine is a Shiva linga (phallus). To the right of the shrine door is Gajalaksmi, holding a lotus and a fruit, being bathed by four elephants. There are also two male attendants (ayudha-purushas) with water pitchers holding a conch, a discus (chakra) and a lotus, which are the attributes of Vishnu. On the right wall of the vestibule is Kartikeya, the son of Shiva, holding a fowl, a trident, and a lotus and nearby is a peacock, his mount. Amourous couples are carved on the pillars of the vestibule.

Antechamber of the shrine

On the south side of the back wall, the first panel depicts the *Lingodbhava murti* Shiva. The story goes that once Vishnu and Brahma were arguing how one of them was greater than the other. Then suddenly, a column of fire, in the form of Shiva-linga, emerged between them. Vishnu assumed the form of a boar and went down to trace its bottom while Brahma, in the form of a swan, flew up to find its top. But neither of them succeeded. The story emphasises that Shiva is the supreme god. The panel depicts Brahma on the left and Vishnu on the right, both worshiping Shiva in the middle.

Next is a panel showing Shiva as *Tripurari*, killing the demon Tripurasura. Shiva holds a bow, an arrow, a sword and a shield in four of his eight hands. He is riding a four-horse chariot driven by Brahma. According to the story in the *Mahabharata*, the sons of Tripurasura obtained from Brahma a boon that their three forts will come together only once in hundred years, and then only can they be destroyed by an arrow. It was Shiva, who finally destroyed them.

1. As in the north wall, corresponding sculptures are also carved

in the south (right) wall, with Vaishnava themes delineating five of the ten incarnations (*avatara*) of Vishnu. The first shows Krishna lifting Mount Govardhana. Krishna is an incarnation of Vishnu that he assumed to protect the cows of the Vraja (Mathura region).

2. The next shows Vishnu as Narayana reclining on Shesha, which has a human head and five hoods. From the god's navel has emerged a lotus on which is seated Brahma. Lakshmi, the consort of Vishnu, is sitting at her lord's feet and there are seven figures below.

3. This shows Vishnu on an eagle (*garuda*), his mount. Garuda is shown in a human form.

4. This is an unfinished sculpture, probably a later attempt to carve out a lingam.

5. Vishnu in the form of a boar (Varaha) holding earth (Prithvi) in his hand; there are snakes below.

6. This is the dwarf (Vamana) incarnation of Vishnu, as Trivikrama. He has eight hands holding a sword, a club, an arrow, a discus (*chakra*), a shield, and a bow. His left leg is lifted towards heaven and on his right is the dwarf Vamana, with an umbrella. Near him is Shukra, the preceptor of demons, and to the left are an eagle, Vishnu's mount, and king Bali. According to the Puranic legend, Bali was a great devotee of Vishnu. Once, when he was performing a sacrifice, Vishnu went to him and asked for some land as donation. Bali agreed and Vishnu, in his Vamana (dwarf) incarnation, encompassed the three worlds—earth, heaven, and the nether-world—in three strides. Hence he is known as Trivikrama.

Aesthetically, this is one of the finest composition in Indian art, noted for its diagonalism and the feeling of charging emotion.

7. The man-lion incarnation of Vishnu (Narsimha): he holds a battle-axe (*parashu*) and a conch (*shankha*) **[Fig. 5.2]**. He has caught the demon Hiranyakashipu with his three hands as he destroys him. This is perhaps a most dynamic representation of its class, marked by a delicate balance. It can be described as a frozen tableau. The artist has succeeded in rendering a three dimensional effect.

Cave 16

Architecturally, and sculpturally, this is undoubtedly the finest cave temple in the world. Locally known as Kailas, it can better be

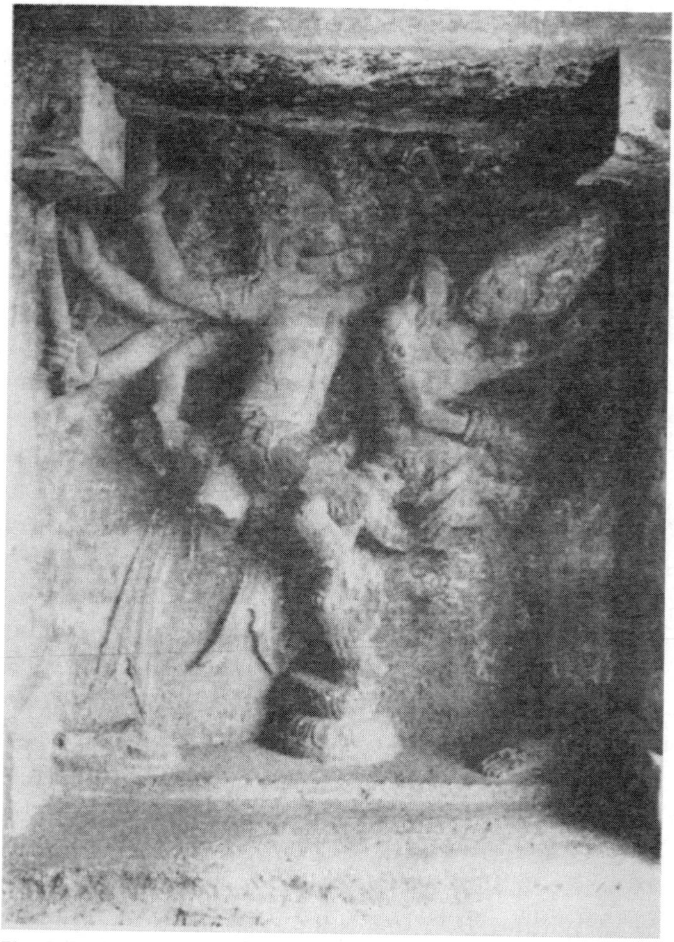

Fig. 5.2. Cave 15 (Dashavatara), upper floor, Narsimha fighting Hiranyakashipu.

described as a monolithic shrine—an architectural sculpture. It is to a great extent a copy of the Virupaksha temple at Pattadakal (Karnataka) but twice its size **[Figs. 5.3–4–5]**.

It was carved under the patronage of king Krishna I (757–72) of the Rashtrakuta dynasty, as is evident from the Baroda copper plate grant of king Karkka II of the Gujarat branch of Rashtrakutas, which is dated to 812–13 AD.

The Baroda plates narrate an interesting story. The gods, once

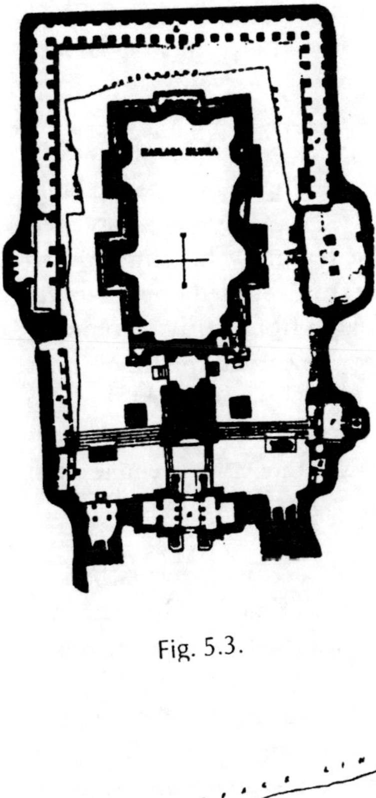

Fig. 5.3.

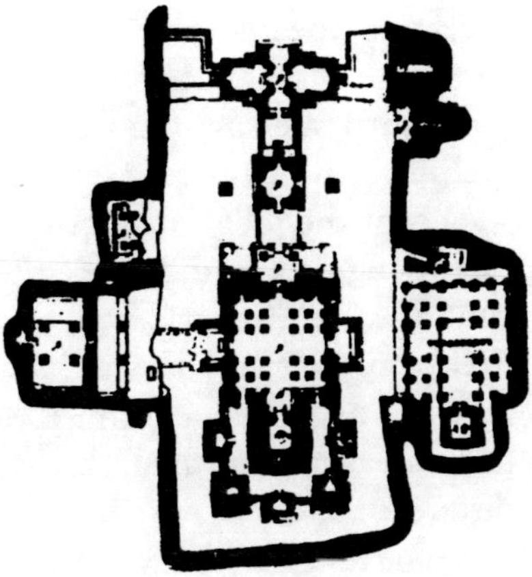

Fig. 5.4.

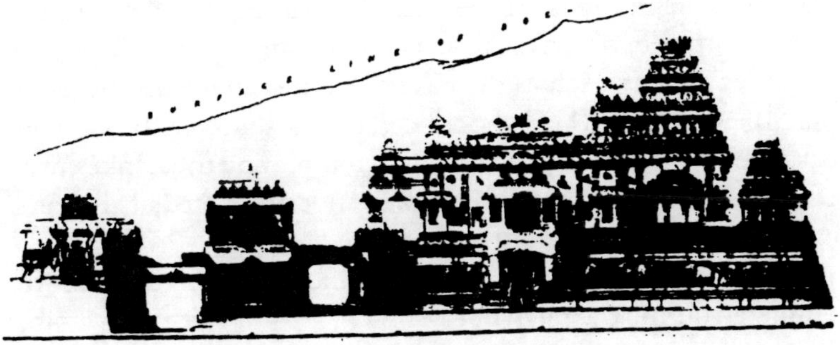

Fig. 5.5.

Fig. 5.3. Plan of Cave 16 (Kailas), main temple, ground floor.
Fig. 5.4. Plan of Cave 16 (Kailas), main temple, upper floor.
Fig. 5.5. Cave 16 (Kailas), elevation.

while travelling in their celestial vehicles, saw the Kailas temple from above. They said, 'This abode of Svayambhu Shiva cannot be man-made'. Even the architect of the temple himself was astonished; and confessed that even with utmost perseverance, he would not be able to accomplish such a task again.

According to a legend in the *Katha-kalpa-taru* (dated to the tenth century AD), which has survived in mediaeval Marathi literature, the queen of the Rashtrakuta king Elu wanted to build a magnificent temple of Shiva and vowed that she would not touch food until she saw the finial of the temple. The king invited architects from different regions but they expressed their inability to accept the job. One architect Kokasa from Paithan, which is nearby, agreed to undertake the task. He carved the finial in no time and the queen had to give up her fast. This was possible because in cave excavations, the work always starts from the top and proceeds downwards. In Maharashtra, those who cannot enter a temple often prostrate before the finial (kalasha) over the spire (shikhara) from a distance.

The Kailas complex consists of a number of monuments, besides the main cave, which is popularly know as Kailas or Ramgamahal because of the paintings in it. The Kailas itself has five subsidiary shrines around its sanctum (garbha-griha) in the circumambulatory path (pradakshina-patha), besides the Nandi pavilion and the Gopura entrance, which too form part of the main shrine. There are also other shrines, such as the River Goddess chapel in the north court, the *Yajna-shala* (Hall of sacrifice), the Paralanka in the southern rock face, the gallery around the main temple and the Lankeshwar. All these shrines and the Kailasa were not excavated at the same time but belong to different periods.

The Kailas is a gigantic edifice which in all likelihood was completed during the reign of Krishna I (757–72) although doubts have been expressed whether such a huge monument could have been carved out in a short period of fifteen years **[Fig. 5.6]**.

Temple complex—Gopura

The temple is situated on the ground level and has a high rock-cut screen at the front, on which are carved sculptures, mostly the *dikpalas* (guardians of directions), besides other divinities. Many of these,

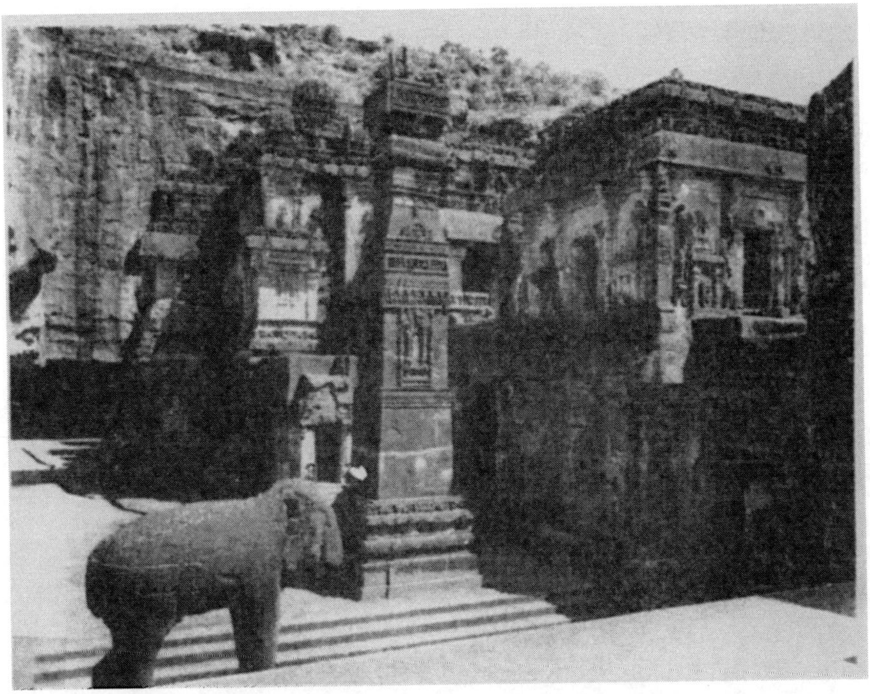

Fig. 5.6. Cave 16 (Kailas), general view of north court.

however, are badly mutilated. From the north, in the first panel, only the outline can be seen incised, the second has Shiva with ten hands, while the third shows a Brahma, but both these appear to be unfinished. On the western side of the wall is the Lingodbhava-murti, which emphasises Shiva's superiority over Vishnu and Brahma who are seen flanking the lingam in the centre. Next is a four armed Shiva holding a trident (trishula). The following two figures are completely damaged while the next is unfinished. Then there is Kartikeya on his mount, a peacock. There is a band above the fourth and the seventh panels in which a *Mahabharata* episode has been carved. On the left is Arjuna in the guise of a mendicant and in the next scene he is shown abducting Subhadra. The battle between Arjuna and Balarama, Subhadra's brother, who is shown holding a plough, his distinguishing symbol, is also depicted.

The next three figures are Agni on a ram, Vayu on a stag and Varuna on a crocodile. They are the guardians of directions (dikpalas). In Hindu mythology, there are eight dikpalas. In the corner formed by the screen wall and the back wall of the entrance gate is a finely carved naga (cobra) couple with a female dwarf. On the entrance, on the left is Ganga on a crocodile and on the right is Yamuna on a tortoise. They are the river goddesses.

On the right side, next to Yamuna, is a naga couple like that on the left. In the following panel is Indra with his consort Indrani on an elephant. Next is Yama, god of death, on buffalo. They are the two guardian deities of the east and the south. Then there is a Vishnu in his *varaha* (boar) incarnation (*avatara*): Nri-varaha, as he is shown in human form. There is a Vishnu on a *garuda* (eagle) on the north face of the screen. Next is Vishnu, again as a Vamana (*dwarf*), also known as Trivikrama because he covered the three worlds in three strides. The next two panels, showing Shiva dancing and the man-lion (Narsimha) incarnation of Vishnu, are damaged. The last shows Shiva dancing the Tandava; its lower part destroyed and with flying Vidyadharas in the upper part.

The entrance gateway, flanked by a Ganga and a Yamuna, has a projecting balcony above it, and is crowned by a vaulted roof, having a chaitya window on either end, supported by males. Two of the central finials have sockets for flag poles. In the eastern arch is an *Ardhanari* Shiva (male–female); in the western side is a Shiva carrying his lingam and by his side is Parvati. In the southern arch is Brahma holding a water vessel, a book, a rosary and a ladle, while in the northern arch is a carved Vishnu.

The gopuram (entrance gateway) is double storeyed and a passage is provided through its lower part for entering the temple. On passing through the gateway, we find a chamber on either side on a raised platform. Its squarish pillars have vase and foliage (ghata-pallava) capitals. On either side of the entrance are the lords of wealth, Shankhanidhi on the left and Padmanidhi on the right, holding their attributes, a conch and a lotus, with bags of money from which coins are flowing out. Further, inside the portico is a Ganesha on the left and Durga mahishasuramardini on the right.

On entering through the portico, one finds two courts on either side of the temple—on the north and the south—and sculptures on the interior of the screen wall. The first is Durga slaying the buffalo demon, which is one of the finest of its class **[Fig. 5.7]**. The goddess

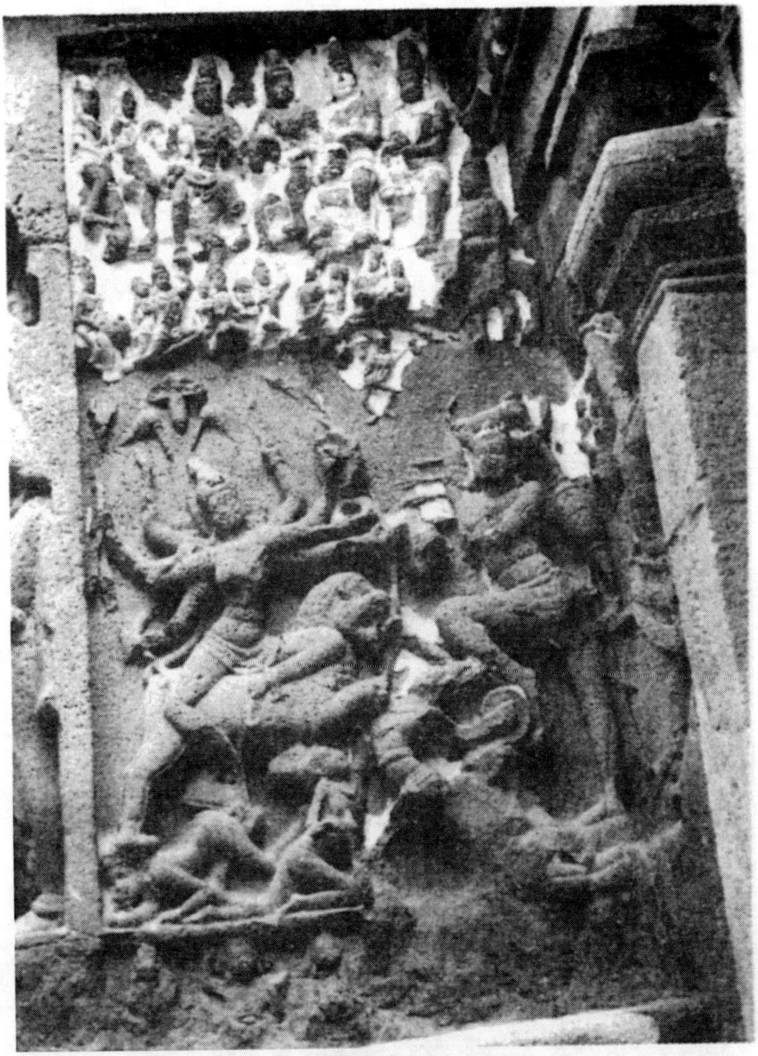

Fig. 5.7. Cave 16 (Kailas), Durga in the north court.

is eight-armed, holding different weapons, and riding a lion who is shown pouncing on the demon. There are gods above in the sky, which include Indra, Vayu, Yama, Agni, Kubera, and Varuna on their respective mounts in the upper row, while in the lower row are Ishana and Ishwara, both on bulls. Flying Vidyadharas are also present. It may be noted that the *Durga-sapta-shati*, a sacred text, states that the Lokapalas were present when the goddess destroyed the demon Mahishasura. Stylistically, this panel is very similar to that at Mahabalipuram (Tamil Nadu).

The next panel depicts Krishna lifting mount Govardhan. The sculpture (sixth from left) is of iconographical interest. It shows Kama, the god of love (or Madana) and his consort, Rati. Kama holds a sugarcane in his left hand, above which flutters his flag (makaradhvaja) **[Fig. 5.8]**. Next to him is Vishnu followed by Lakshmi.

In the south court too there were sculptures on the interior of

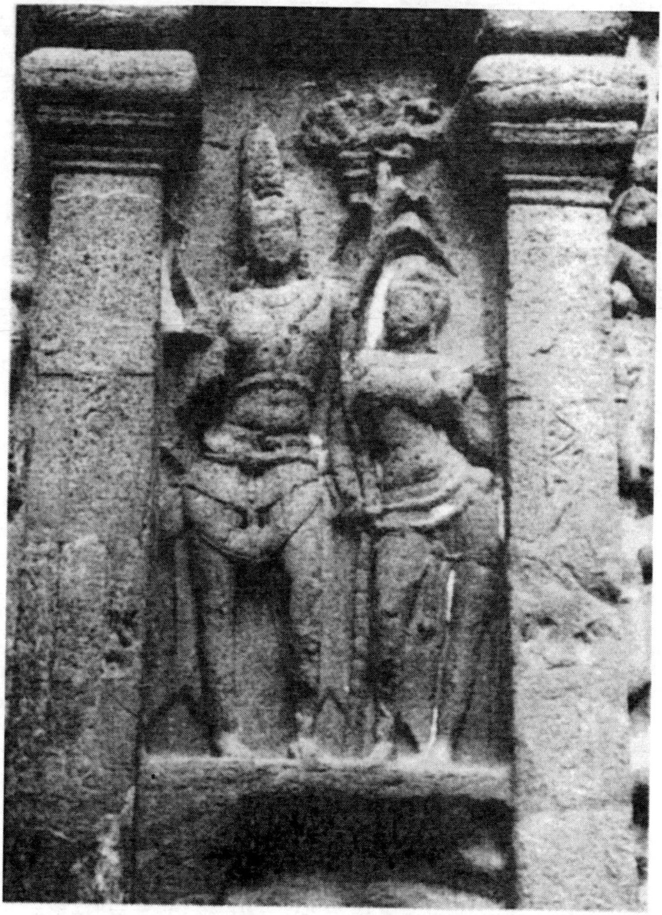

Fig. 5.8. Cave 16 (Kailas), Madana or Kama and Rati in the north court.

the screen wall, but only a few of them now survive. The most noteworthy is that in the north-west corner depicting Shiva killing the demon Tripurasura. Shiva's chariot is driven by the four-headed Brahma **[Fig. 5.9]**. The god is shown taking out an arrow from the quiver on his back with his right hand; and in his left hand he holds a bow. According to a story in the *Mahabharata*, the demons obtained a boon from Brahma who told them that they could be killed only by Shiva. Assisted by other gods, Shiva prepared an arrow which was actually nothing but Vishnu himself; Agni became its barb and

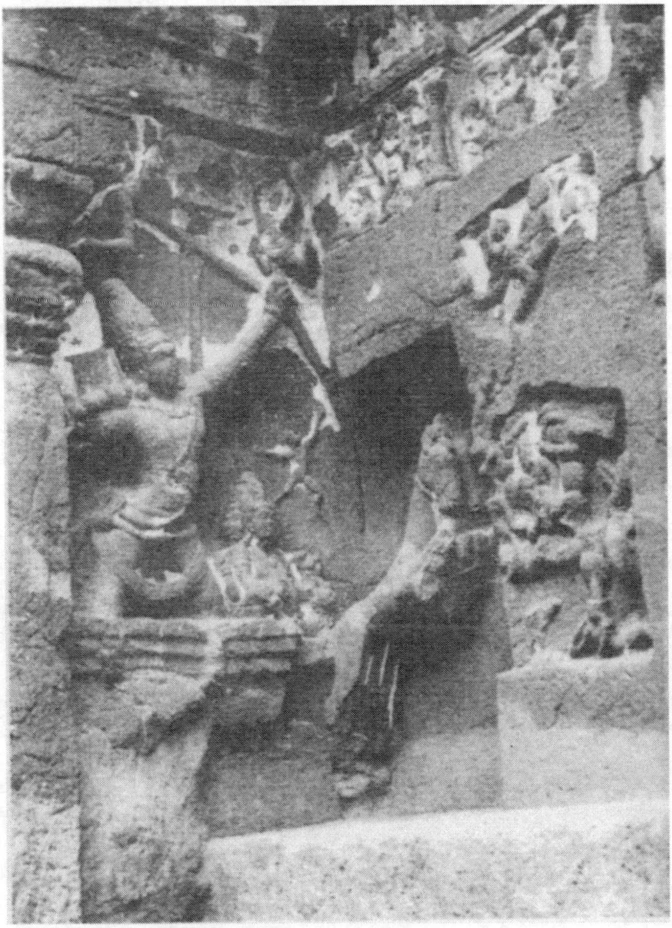

Fig. 5.9. Cave 16 (Kailas), Tripurari Shiva in the south court.

Yama its feather. Shiva made the Vedas his bow, Brahma his chariot, and killed the three demons.

On the left is Bhairava, a gruesome form of Shiva. According to a legend in the *Puranas*, Shiva was once insulted by Brahma, and he therefore cut off one of Brahma's four heads. But that head stuck to Shiva's hand. He had therefore to wander for twelve years as a Kapalika and then the head fell at Varanasi at the spot which is now known as Kapala-mochana. There are four more panels on the left of which the first two are male figures, the third is a dancing Shiva and the fourth probably depicts Shiva killing Andhakasura. Further left there are two unfinished panels and the last one shows Shiva-Parvati. After this, on the south, is an unfinished excavation as in the north court.

A rock bridge joins the entrance gate and the double-storied Nandi *mandapa*. Under this bridge, on the western wall, is a huge Gajalakshmi, seated on a lotus and being bathed by elephants **[Fig. 5.10]**. Over her head is an umbrella, with Vidyadharas flying in

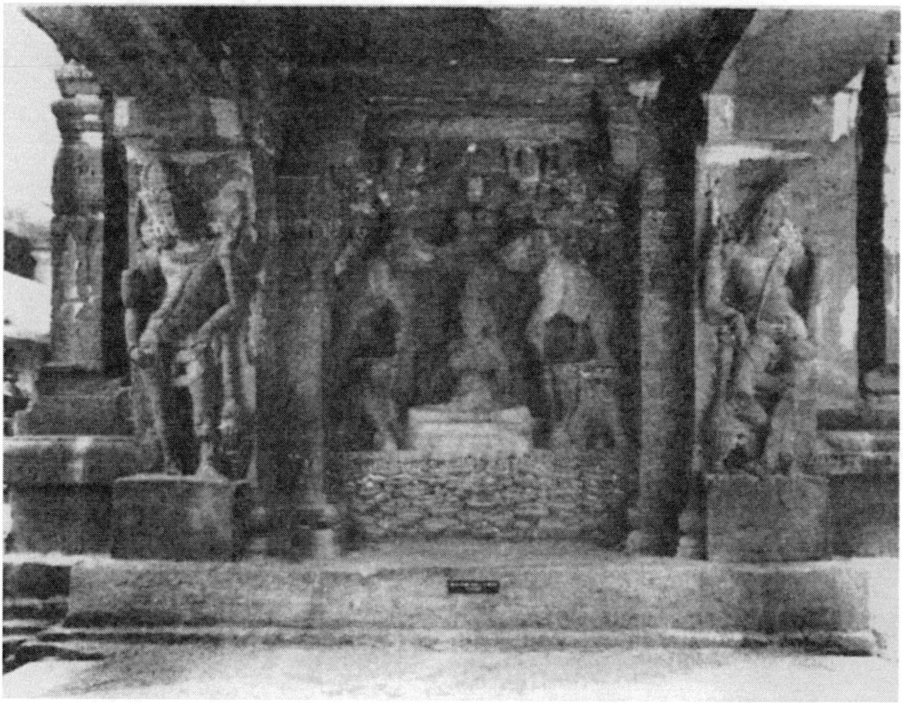

Fig. 5.10. Cave 16 (Kailas), Gajalakshmi, facing entrance.

the sky. Her face is mutilated. There are traces of an eighth-century inscription on her seat, which records that the image of the goddess was a gift from one Bhadrankura of the Radhe family.

There are two gigantic compositions under the rock bridge opposite each other. On the eastern face is Shiva slaying the demon Andhaka **[Fig. 5.11]**. Shiva is ten-armed, of which four support the elephant hide over his head, while the remaining hands hold a damaru (an hour-glass shaped small drum), a trident, an elephant tusk, and a bowl; one hand is touching the face of Parvati. Below his right leg is the dwarf demon (apasmara-purusha). Between his legs, dwarfs (ganas) and Bhringi are seen dancing with joy. Bhringi is standing

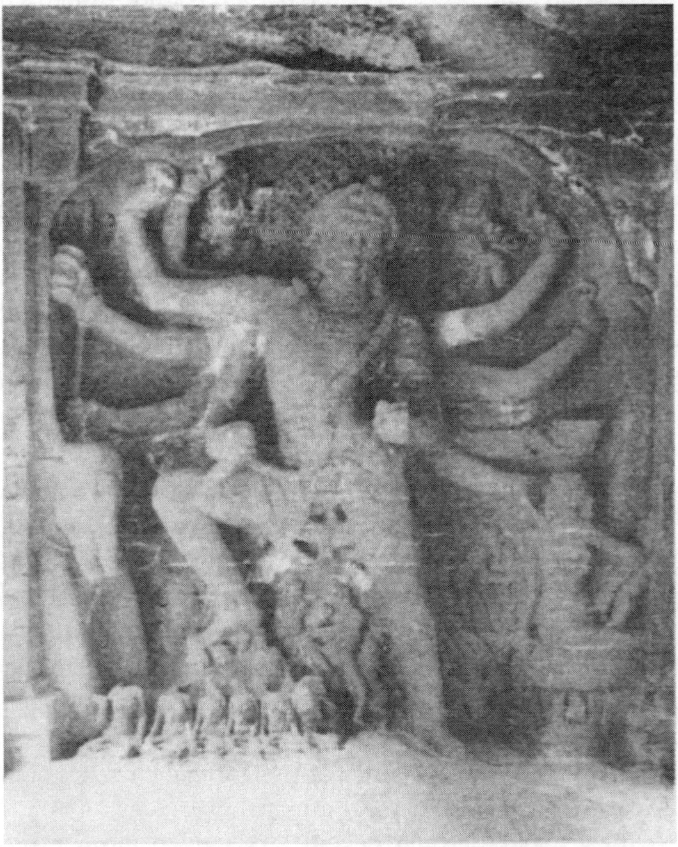

Fig. 5.11. Cave 16 (Kailas), Andhakasura-vadha-murti Shiva, below Nandi-mandapa, on east wall.

near Parvati. Shiva wears a garland of skulls (runda-mala) in the *vajnopavita* (sacred thread) fashion. His matted locks (jata-mukuta) are dishevelled. The elephant head of demon Gajasura is seen on the left below which are sapta-matrikas (seven mother goddesses) with their mounts. According to the Puranic story, a demon, in the form of an elephant, Gajasura, used to harass the brahmins of Varanasi while they were worshipping a Shiva-*linga*. Hence Shiva killed Gajasura and wore his elephant skin. In another story we are told that Andhakasura, who was granted boons by Brahma because of his severe penance, became very powerful and caused trouble to the gods. Shiva therefore had to kill him. But Andhaka had been granted a boon that from every drop of blood falling from his body, a new demon would come to life. In order to prevent this, the gods sent their *shaktis* (consorts) to collect the blood dropping from the demon's body. Shiva then slayed Gajasura, Andhaka's friend, first and then Andhaka. This panel is one of the most impressive because of the sheer force that the artist has successfully delineated.

The opposite panel, in sharp contrast, depicts a benign form of Shiva as *mahayogi* **[Fig. 5.12]**. The god is shown seated on a lotus supported by lions. He is performing penance with his eyes closed in deep meditation. There are gods above; while on the right is Varuna on a crocodile, Vayu on a deer, Mahesha and Ishana on a bull; and on the left are Indra on an elephant, Yama on a buffalo, Agni on a ram and Kubera on a dead body (nara-vahana). These are the guardian deities (*dikpalas*).

On the northern face of the Nandi *mandapa* is Shiva dancing to the accompaniment of music. Although partly destroyed, the panel is noteworthy for its movement and vigour. On the southern face is the man-lion (Nrisimha) incarnation of Vishnu killing Hiranyakashipu. With his left leg, the god is trampling upon Hiranyakashipu and with his right hand he is about to hurl the demon into the sky. Flanking this panel are amorous couples (*mithunas*) in niches. Their occurrence in early mediaeval temples is in all probability due to the influence of the Tantric cult in which the female principle (*shakti*) is predominant.

In the spacious courts on the north and south of the main temple, one is awed by the huge elephants and the victory pillars (dhvaja-

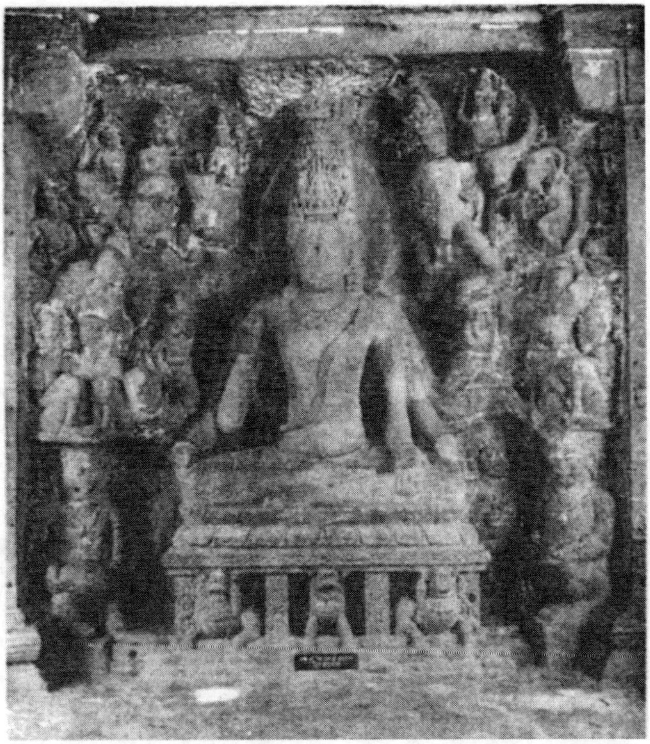

Fig. 5.12. Cave 16 (Kailas), Mahayogi Shiva in the passage connecting Nandi-mandapa to the main temple.

stambha). The massive elephants stand on pedestals. The one in the south is mutilated.

The huge victory pillars, about 16 m high, stand on a higher level. They are both identical, squarish with a cushion capital and a flat abacus. The shaft is carved with broad decorative bands containing kirti-mukhas (lion-like faces) with pearl strings issuing from them and forming festoons. The central band contains human couples, one of them in a copulating posture. Above the decorative bands is a chaitya arch.

Main Temple

The main temple stands on a high, massive plinth on which are carved huge outsize elephants and lions, some of them in combat

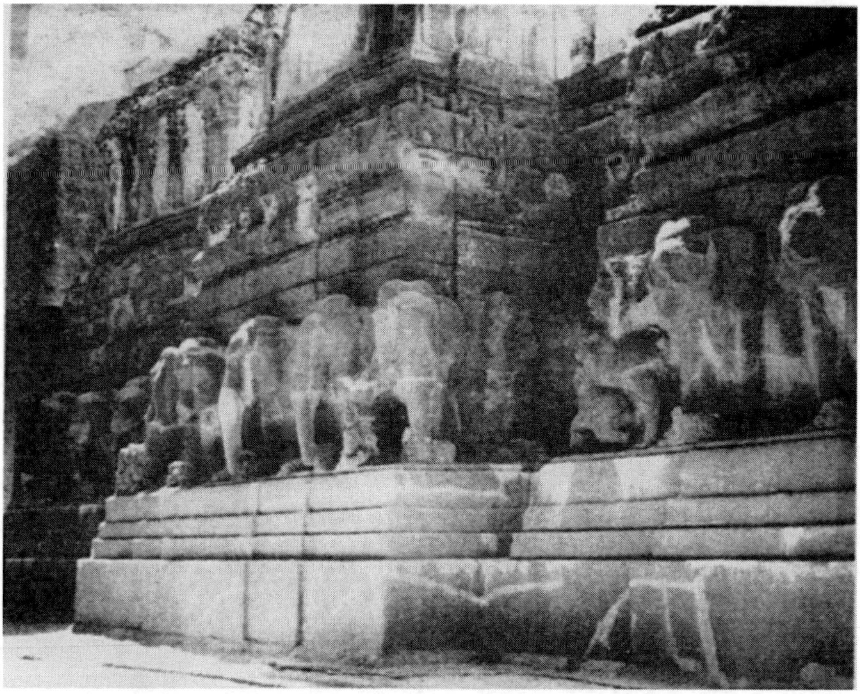

Fig. 5.13. Cave 16 (Kailas), elephants supporting the temple.

[Fig. 5.13]. The temple consists of a sanctum (*garbha-griha*), a vestibule (antarala), a hall (sabha mandapa), an entrance portico (mukha-mandapa) on the west; porches on either side (ardha-mandapas) and a Nandi mandapa at the front. All these have towers (shikharas) of the Dravidian order, which are characterised by receding tiers. The main *shikhara* is crowned by a domical member (stupi). At the base is a small vaulted roof over the vestibule and over the roof is the finial (kalasha) in the centre with two lions (vyala) in combat.

On the northern face of the vaulted roof is a chaitya crowned by a kirti-mukha that contains Shiva in meditation (Mahayogi) with flying figures on either side and elephants and mythical creatures at the base. The roof of the sanctum is flat and has a lotus crowned by a finial (*kalasha*) around which are four mythical lions (*vyalas*) in four cardinal directions. The roof of the entrance portico is also flat but over it are carved lotuses in receding tires.

The external walls of the temple are divided into panels containing exquisite sculptures. The most important and artistic is that on the south, which depicts Ravana shaking Mount Kailas, a common theme at Ellora **[Fig. 5.14]**. It is a very large sculpture, far superior to similar ones found in other caves. It is very realistically

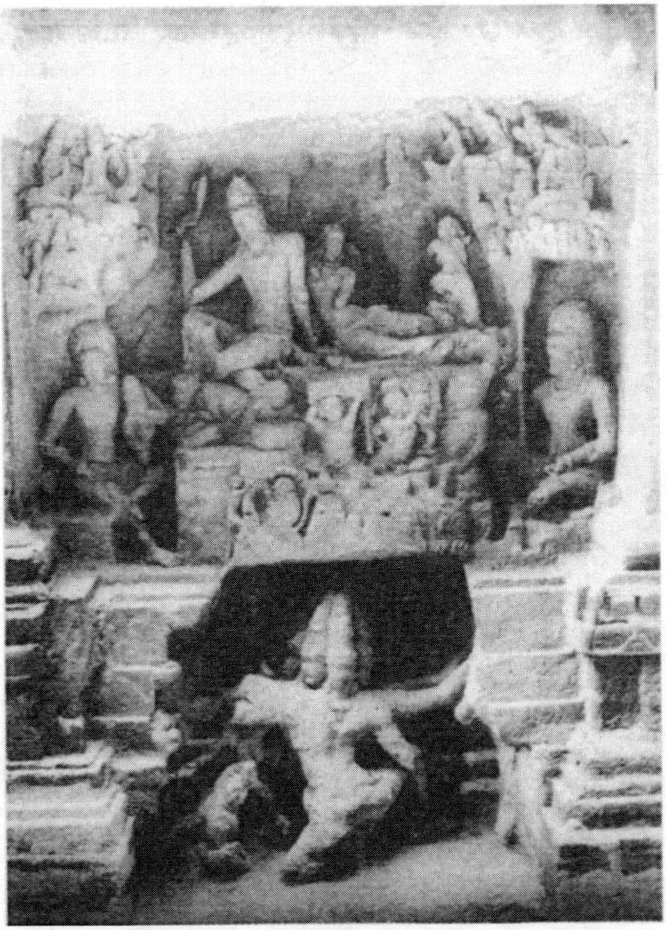

Fig. 5.14. Cave 16 (Kailas), Ravana shaking Kailas, on the southern face.

portrayed: a frightened Parvati clutching Shiva's arm, and a panic stricken maid running. Shiva, however, is composed, and he is about to crush Ravana with his left toe. Unfortunately, many of Ravana's heads and hands are mutilated and so also is the lower half of his body. The entire panel is characterised by energy and movement and has been hailed as the finest representation of the theme.

The basement of the hall of the temple is carved with epic scenes; the *Mahabharata* on the north and the *Ramayana* on the south. The former are carved in five bands and the first two rows illustrate the *Kiratarjuniya* story. Starting from the left hand corner, Arjuna is first shown in penance, and then the fight between him and Shiva over the hunted boar is depicted. Shiva is then pleased and gives the Pasupata missile to Arjuna. Next is the *Mahabharata* war with chariots. In the third row is Abhimanyu entering the *chakra-vyuha* (circular arrangement of army). The war continues in the fourth row and in the fifth are Arjuna and his charioteer, Krishna.

Scenes from Krishna's life are depicted in the last two rows. Starting from right, Krishna's birth is shown in Kamsa's prison. In the next Kamsa, Krishna's maternal uncle, is trying to kill Krishna by hurling him in the sky. Further left is Putana, the ogress who wanted to kill Krishna by feeding him her poisonous milk. Krishna's childhood pranks, such as stealing butter, are shown on the extreme left. As punishment, Krishna is tied to a mortar. Among Krishna's deeds, we see him killing Narakasura, who comes in the guise of a bird, and his combat with a lion. Finally, he is seen killing Kamsa, whose chariot is broken.

The *Ramayana* scenes are carved on the south side in eight rows. In the first row from right, we see Rama's departure from Ayodhya; Rama is shown touching the feet of Dasharatha, his father, and Sita is standing by his side. Rama, Lakshman, and Sita are being given farewell by the residents of Ayodhya. In the left corner they are seen crossing a river in a boat.

In the second row, the scene starts from the left. First is Rama's meeting with Bharata and Shurpanakha, who has come to lure Rama, but her nose is cut by Lakshman. The following row begins from the right; it depicts the story of Maricha, who has come in the guise of a golden deer. Rama and Lakshman pursue the deer, then Ravana, who comes in guise of a mendicant, carries away Sita.

In the next scene, Jatayu the bird is seen attacking Ravana, who cuts its beak. The wounded bird informs Rama about Sita's abduction.

In the next panel are seen Rama, Lakshman, Hanuman, and Sugriva. In the forth row, in which the story begins from the left, we see the fight between Vali and Sugriva. The chief of the monkeys, Vali, is killed and Rama is consoling his two wives, Ruma and Tara. Then Sugriva becomes the king of the monkeys; his coronation is attended by Rama, Lakshman, and the monkeys.

In the fifth now, starting from the left, are Rama and Sugriva followed by Samprati, the brother of Jatayu, bringing information about Sita. Hanuman is on the mountain going to Lanka. He is then shown entering the mouth of an ogress and coming out of her belly.

The sixth panel shows Sita in Ashoka *vana* (forest) surrounded by ogresses. Hanuman is brought before Ravana. The following row is damaged. It probably depicts Rama and monkeys building a bridge. In the last row, the battle between Rama and Ravana is shown. In this, Rama emerges victorious.

The hall (sabha-mandapa) is squarish and is supported by 16 pillars, four groups of four pillars each dividing the hall into cubicles. The pillars with squarish shafts are intricately carved with a variety of motifs and depictions of stories from the Puranas and are crowned by vase-and-foliage capitals **[Fig. 5.15]**. Some of them are carved with erotic couples. The ceiling of the hall was once adorned with paintings and the cave is therefore also known as Rang-mahal. On the beam, near the southern balcony, is a painted Shiva dancing **[Fig. 5.16]**. In the centre, on the ceiling is also carved a dancing Shiva. He is eight-armed and is accompanied by Parvati, who is standing on a lotus.

In the vestibule joining the hall and the sanctum, a Soma-Skanda panel is carved on the southern wall. It shows Shiva, Parvati and Skanda (Kartikeya) with Shiva *ganas* (dwarfs) below. The opposite wall shows Shiva and Parvati playing *chausar*. On the ceiling of the vestibule is carved a goddess who has been identified as Annapurna; with Brahma and Vishnu flanking her. The entrance door to the sanctum (*garbha-griha*) is very elegantly decorated but much of it is covered by the lime plaster which was applied in the

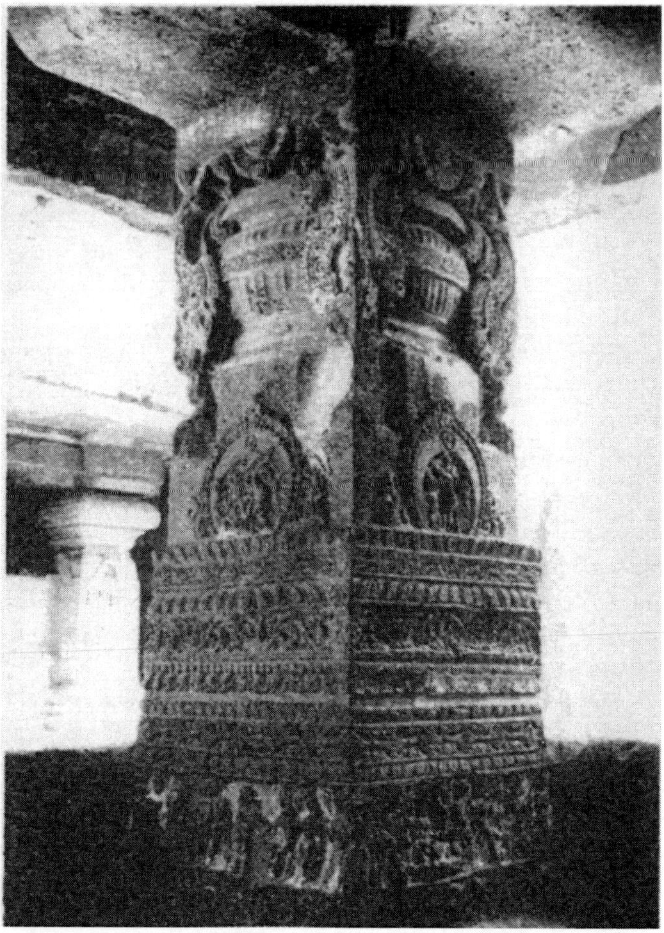

Fig. 5.15. Cave 16 (Kailas), a pillar in the northern balcony.

mediaeval times. The doorway has Ganga on the left and Yamuna on the right, but their heads have been chopped off **[Fig. 5.17]**.

The Shiva *linga* in the sanctum was badly mutilated. It was formerly richly ornamented with rubies and hence the name of the cave—Manakeshwar—which occurs in mediaeval Marathi literature.

The hall (*sabha-mandapa*) is rather dark, with six small windows tastefully decorated with floral and arabesque patterns and sometimes with animal motifs.

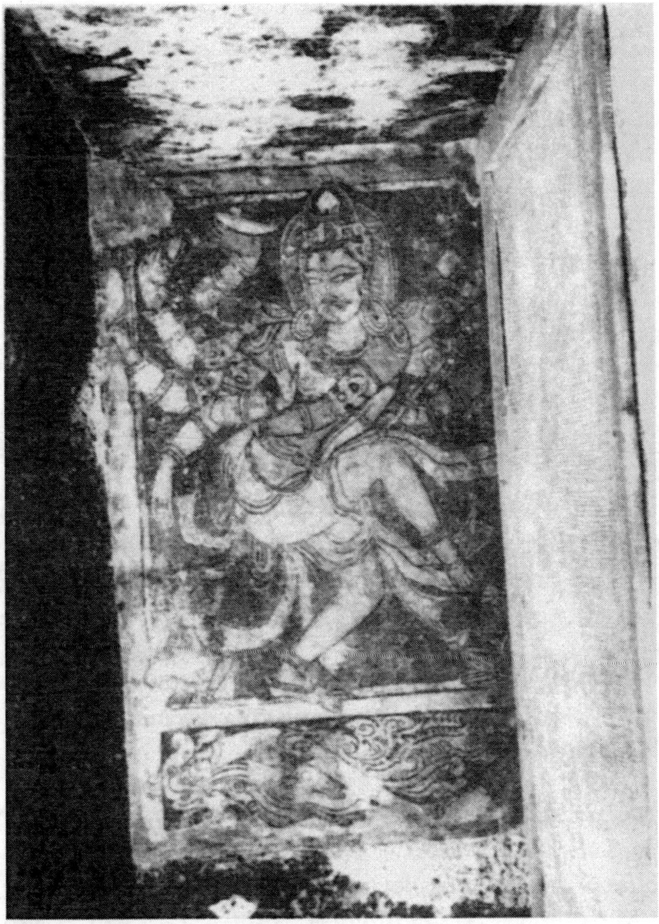

Fig. 5.16. Cave 16 (Kailas), Shiva dancing, a painting in the hall.

The five subsidiary shrines around the sanctum on the outer side make Kailas a *panchayatana* shrine. They are located in the circumambulatory passage but presently they do not contain any images and one cannot therefore say anything about their sectarian affiliations.

The exterior walls of the temple are profusely adorned with sculptured panels. Near the northern staircase is a panel showing Ravana shaking Mount Kailas. On the other side, near the southern

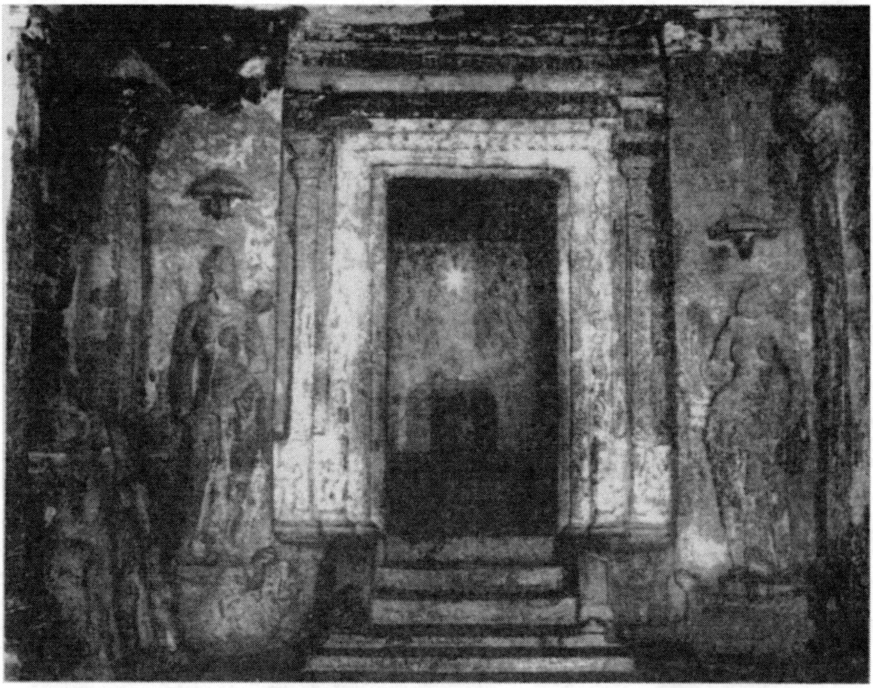

Fig. 5.17. Cave 16 (Kailas), sanctum with Ganga-Yamuna flanking entrance.

staircase, is Brahma with attendants. On the way up by the northern staircase, midway on the western wall of the temple is Shiva protecting young Markandeya from Yama, the god of death **[Fig. 5.18]**. Markandeya is clutching the *lingam* out of which Shiva is emerging and is about to thrust his trident into Yama's body. By the side of this panel is Shiva as Gangadhara, with the Ganga emerging through his matted locks (jata-mukuta) **[Fig. 5.19]**. The stream is seen falling over Janhu, who is seated on the left from where it widens and rushes down upon the sons of Sagara, to bring them back to life. Bhagirath, a devotee of Shiva who performed a penance for this, is seen kneeling before Shiva. Corresponding this, on the southern side, is the *Lingodbhava-murti* of Shiva **[Fig. 5.20]**. Next is Brahma.

On the northern wall of the temple is a panel showing Durga killing the buffalo demon. This sculpture can be seen from the

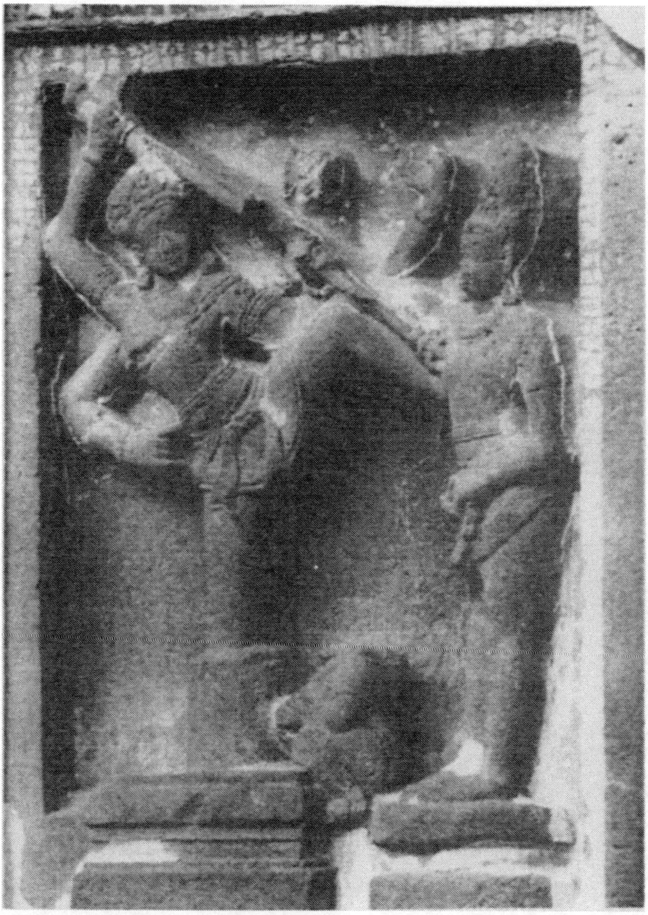

Fig. 5.18. Cave 16 (Kailas), exterior of the main temple, north-west corner, Shiva protecting Markandeya from Yama.

northern balcony of the hall, which has guardians on either side. Similarly, on the southern wall is Lakulisha, who is shown standing with a club (*laguda*) in his right hand. To the right of this is a small panel which portrays Sita's abduction by Ravana, who is carrying her in his chariot. Jatayu attempts to prevent it. Ravana is about to kill the bird with his sword. Next to this, on the right, the fight between Vali and Sugriva, which is described in the *Ramayana*, is

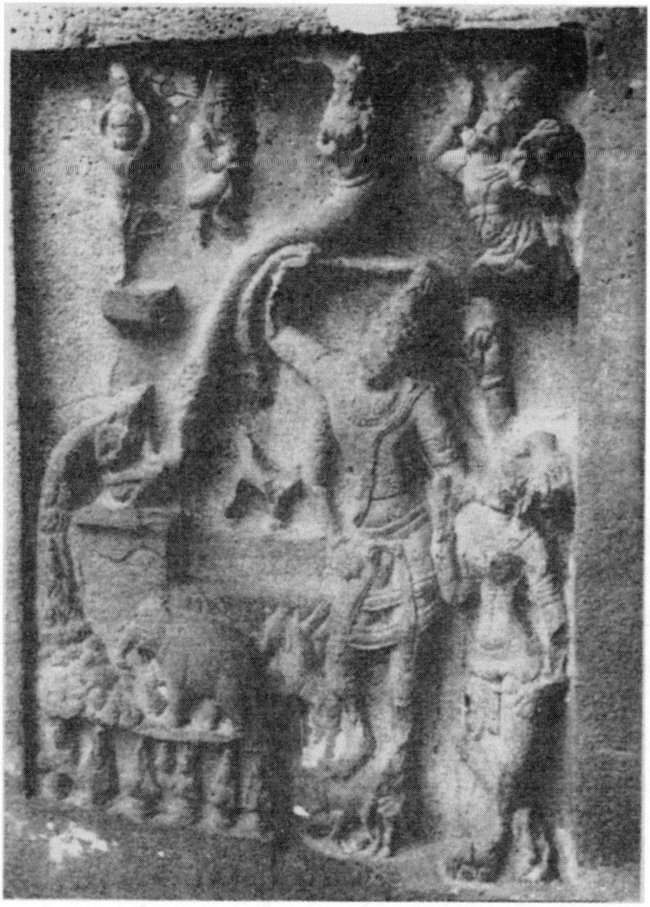

Fig. 5.19. Cave 16 (Kailas), exterior of main temple, north-west corner, Shiva as Gangadhar.

shown. Sugriva killed Vali, and Rama with Lakshman behind him, is consoling Tara, Vali's wife. This panel is followed by Narisimha killing Hiranyakashipu. Higher up on the south wall is a Gandharva couple with musical instruments.

Paintings

The temple was embellished with paintings on its walls, which have only survived in fragments in the entrance portico. In the north-

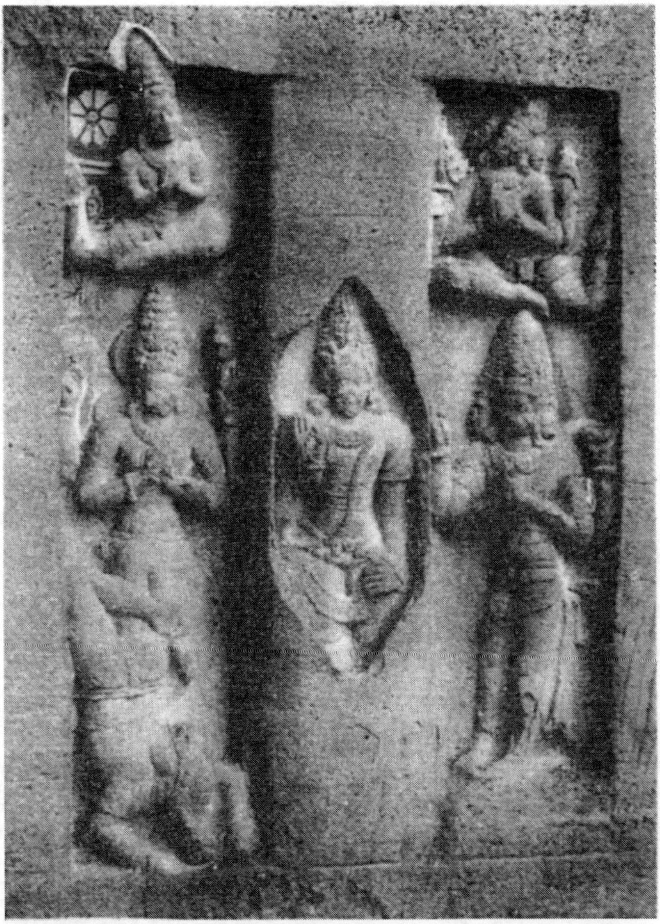

Fig. 5.20. Cave 16 (Kailas), exterior of main temple, south-west corner, Lingodbhava-murti Shiva.

western part is shown a person, probably a deity, riding a mythical animal (*shardula*). He wears elaborate jewellery. There are some male and female figures around him, probably devotees. Above, in a squarish panel, are two baby elephants playing in a lotus pond. A dwarf is riding one of the elephants. Stylistically the painting is in the Ajanta tradition and is contemporary with the temple (eighth century).

In another panel is shown Shiva in the centre with Parvati on

Nandi on the left and Kartikeya on a peacock on the right with umbrellas over their heads. In the second layer of painting is shown Vishnu on *garuda* flying in the sky. This painting is assigned to the tenth century.

The third layer depicts a battle scene showing foot soldiers with lances and shields, warrior on elephants, and horsemen led by their chief riding an elephant. Behind his head are Devanagari characters '*Svasti shri Pramara Ram*', which may refer to a Paramara king, probably Munja, who had invaded the Deccan in the twelfth century.

On the west, over the king's head are letters *Svasti Kannaura devaraya*, which may refer to a Nikumbha king of the twelfth century. On the north side is another king with an army with the inscription *Mahamara loku* i.e. Mohammedans/Muslims, who had started coming to India from the eighth and ninth centuries onward and found employment in the Indian army. The paintings are in the Ajanta tradition. Unfortunately they are in a bad state of preservation.

River Goddess shrine

In the north-west corner of the northern court is a small shrine (6.40 x 2.70 m) dedicated to river goddesses: Ganga, Yamuna and Saraswati. They are carved in niches with pilasters on the sides and a *makara-torana* above. On the left, Saraswati is seen standing on a lotus, in a flexed posture; in the middle is Ganga on a crocodile, and on the right is Yamuna on a tortoise. The figures are slender, in sharp contrast to the robust ones in other shrines, and they appear to be the handiwork of artists from the Pratihara kingdom. The shrine may have been added later in the ninth century. Govind III (794–814), a Rashtrakuta monarch, had invaded the north and defeated the Pratiharas in the Ganga valley and may have brought some Pratihara artists with him.

Hall of Sacrifice (*Yajna-shala*)

This hall is excavated in the southern wall in the south court of Kailas. It is at a higher level and is approached by flighted stairs. At the front, it has two pillars and two pilasters and on each pillar is carved a very elegant female figure. The one on the left, which is better preserved, wears fine jewellery, with a delecate tiara on her head, while her hair is gathered in an elongated knot. Her attendant, a female dwarf, is seen holding a jug in her left hand and to her right is a male dwarf.

The hall is full of exquisite scruptures on all three sides. They include the seven mother goddesses (*Sapta-matrikas*) and Kala, Ganesha and Virabhadra. Starting from the right wall, the first is Durga (or Chandi) on a lion; of her four hands three are broken and in the fourth is a trident. The next is a six-armed goddess, but most of her hands are broken. In one of her right hands she holds a trident while in one of her left hands is a snake and a bowl of sweets; on her seat is a jackal gnawing at the corpse on the floor and she can therefore be identified as Chamunda. In the left corner is Kala, the god of death, with a skeletal body; seated on a corpse and to his right is Kali. This figure of Kala is a most remarkable representation of the god of death.

On the back wall are seven mother goddesses, each with a child. They are accompanied by Ganesha in the left corner. The next is Varahi with her mount, a boar, the third is Indrani with an elephant; the fourth cannot be identified (probably Brahmi); the fifth is Vaishnavi with an eagle, the sixth is Kaumari with a peacock; the seventh is Maheshwari with a bull. Then there is Chamunda, whose mount appears to be a fox or a jackal. Then the last is Virabhadra. In the northern corner is carved an eagle, which was the royal emblem of the Rashtrakutas.

The three female figures in the eastern side appear to be important. They each have only two hands and, therefore, are not divinities **[Fig. 5.21]**. The central figure is flanked by a fly whisk bearer, and may therefore be a royal personage. Her hands and legs are destroyed; she is shown seated on a throne. In all probability she may be a Rashtrakuta queen and the hall was a place of sacrifice, if the two rock cut altars in the cave are any indication. Govinda III (794–814) had successfully carried out conquests in the north and south India and had performed many sacrifices. When Rama performed an Ashvamedha sacrifice after Sita's banishment, her golden image was prepared as she herself was not present. This

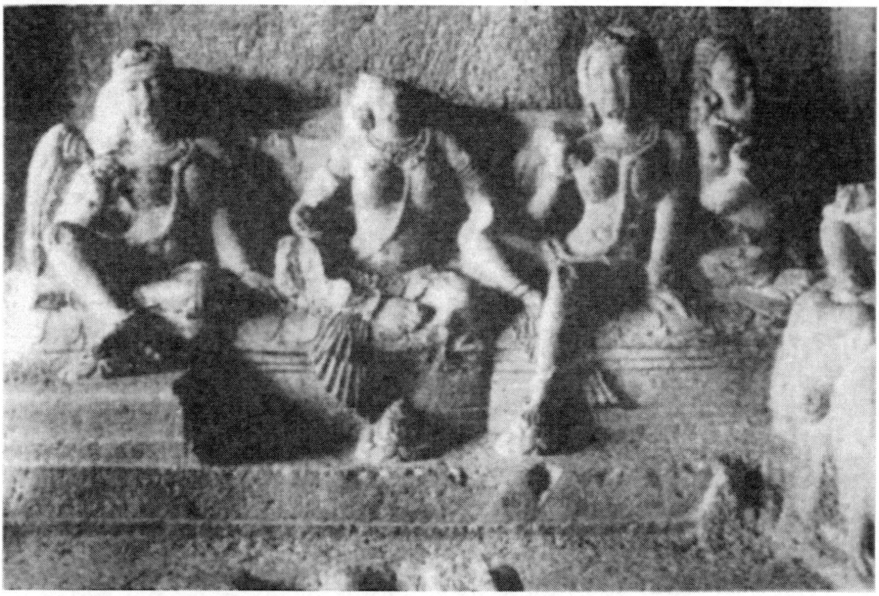

Fig. 5.21. Cave 16 (Kailas), Rashtrakuta queen (?) with female attendants in the *Yajna-shala.*

indicates that the queen plays a very important role in a sacrifice. It is therefore not unlikely that Govinda III's queen was unfortunately not present when he performed the sacrifice, and hence her image was made. The event seems to be represented in the *Yajna-shala* cave.

The *Yajna-shala* is a unique edifice as its sculptures mark the very acme of the Rashtrakuta art. They are carved in the round, which is a rarity in Indian art. They are characterised by a dynamic realism, and the slender yet robust forms show that they have shed their extra weight which marks the earthbound types in Cave 29. The cave is later than the Kailas proper and can be dated to ca. 800 AD.

Paralanka

Further east of *yajna-shala*, in the middle of the southern escarpment, is yet another cave which is known as Paralanka. It is unfortunately unfinished but must have been in the original plan of Kailas to which it was once joined by a rock bridge which is now ruined. It is a four storeyed excavation without any carving or sculpture and may have been used as the residence of artisans who were working on Kailas.

Lankeshwar

In the opposite, northern escarpment, is another cave locally known as Lankeshwar, which is on level with the hall of the main temple. It is approached by a flight of steps where there is a Gajalakshmi panel. The steps lead to a shrine that consists of a Nandi *mandap*, a hall and sanctuary with a circumambulatory path. There is a male divinity with two female attendants near the Nandi *mandap*. The hall contains a few sculptures on its walls and has richly carved pillars with vase-and-foliage capitals. But they are short and stumpy.

Among the sculptures on the left wall, the first is a Ganesha, and the next is Vishnu's Narisimha incarnation in which he is shown tearing out the entrails of the demon Hiranyakashipu. Further, there is the Hindu trinity of Brahma, Vishnu, and Mahesh, with their attendants. After this there is Parvati with a lotus in her hand and near her is Ganesha. Next is the boar (*varaha*) incarnation of Vishnu, protecting the earth. This is followed by Surya (sun god) flanked by devotees. The last panel shows Shiva-Parvati playing *chausar*, with the dwarfs (*ganas*) and Nandi below.

The sanctum has Ganga and Yamuna in the doorway and inside is a Shiva *linga* in the centre: on the back wall is a Trimurti. Of it's three faces, the left is Shiva as creator (*Vamadeva*), the right is Shiva as destroyer (*aghora*): the central one is the protector. On the right wall of the sanctuary is a panel depicting Ravana shaking Mount Kailas. This panel is not very artistic.

The most imposing sculpture in the cave is on the back wall of the right aisle, which shows Shiva dancing the tandava **[Fig. 5.22]**. It is carved in bold relief and is full of vigour and force, so much so that it appears to be bursting out of its frames. The god has six arms holding a *damaru* (a small drum) and a snake in his left hands. His other hands and legs have been destroyed. He stands in a flexed posture, wears sparse jewellery and his matted looks (*jata-mukuta*) are very intricately carved. His third eye on the forehead indicates

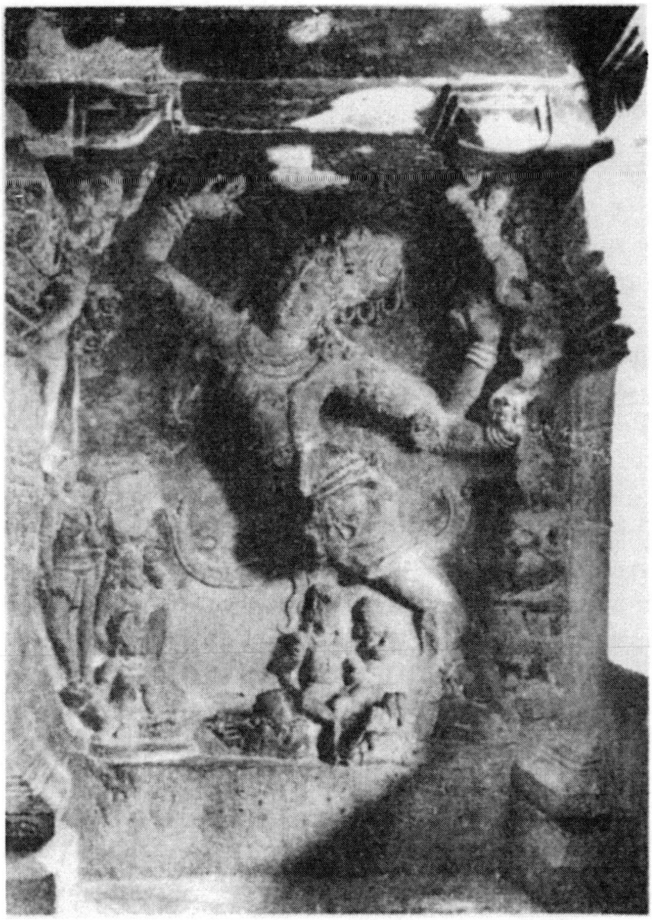

Fig. 5.22. Cave 16 (Kailas), Shiva dancing, in Lankeshwar.

wisdom. He danced tandava at the time of *pralaya* (doomsday), when the world was coming to an end. Near his feet are musicians and a demon whom he has trampled. There are devotees at the bottom and above are flying Vidyadharas. This is the finest image of its class not only at Ellora but in the entire range of Indian art.

On the five pillars on the southern side are carved Shiva Gangadhara, Shiva Parvati, Shiva, Ardhanari Shiva and Durga but they are all mutilated. The cave can be assigned to the early ninth century.

The Galleries

There is a sculpture gallery around the main temples. Starting from below in the northern wall, it continues in the eastern escarpment and ends below Paralanka in the south. It is a pillared corridor with sculptured panels in the back wall. From the north they are:

1. Ravana offering heads to Shiva. Ravana was a great devotee of Shiva and has already offered nine out of ten heads which are seen around a Shiva *linga* below. This story is given in the *Ramayana*, according to which the god appears and prevents the cutting of the tenth head.

2. Shiva-Parvati seated; below is a seated male and a standby female.

3. Shiva and Parvati carrying a *linga*.

4. Similar to no. 3 above but the *linga* is missing.

5. Shiva standing with a bull behind him.

6. Shiva and Parvati with a child.

7. A standing male figure.

8. Probably Ravana shaking Mount Kailas; but the panel is unfinished.

9. Shiva-Parvati seated; Shiva probably holding a *vina* (a stringed instrument).

10. Shiva-Parvati playing dice.

11. Shiva with Rama and Lakshman.

12. Shiva protecting Markandeya from Yama, the god of death.

The following panels are in the eastern gallery, starting from the north:

1. The marriage of Shiva and Parvati (*Kalyana-sundara-murti*); Shiva is holding the hand of Parvati; the priest Brahma is below.

2. Shiva killing the demon Andhakasura.

3. Shiva killing Tripurasura.

4. Shiva-Parvati with Nandi below.

5. Four armed Lakulisha, standing.

6. *Lingodbhava-murti*, *linga* in the centre flanked by Brahma and Vishnu.

7. Gangadhara Shiva, with Ganga in his matted locks.

8. Harihara; a syncretistic image of Shiva and Vishnu in one. According to a Puranic legend, Vishnu once said that he and Shiva

were one. In the panel the left half is Vishnu (Hari) and the right is Shiva (Hara). Shiva holds a trident and Vishnu, a discus (*chakra*) and lotus. To Shiva's right is Nandi and to Vishnu's left is an eagle (*garuda*), their mounts.

9. Vishnu with a devotee.

10. Shiva with Nandi.

11. Brahma.

12. Shiva.

13. Shiva with Nandi.

14. *Bhikshatana-murti* Shiva. Once Shiva cut off one of Brahma's heads and had therefore to beg as mendicant for a year. The panel illustrates this story.

15. Shiva dancing.

16. Shiva Bhairava.

17. Shiva.

18. This too is a rare panel illustrating a Puranic legend. Shiva, in order to test Parvati's resolve to marry him for which she had performed many austerities, assumes the form of a young man and goes to her and begs for food. She tells him to have a bath and finish his ablutions. He goes to the river and shouts that he has been caught by a crocodile. Parvati comes but cannot give him her hand, which is reserved for Shiva only. But finally to save him does so.

19. Shiva-Parvati.

There are twelve panels in the southern gallery.

1. Ardhanari Shiva (half male, half female)

2. Shiva.

3. Ravana uprooting a Shiva *linga*.

4. Narsimha killing Hiranyakashipu.

5. Vishnu on shesha (cobra)

6. Krishna lifting mount Govardhan to protect cows in Gokul.

7. Vishnu as Vamana.

8. Vishnu on *garuda* (eagle) who is shown in human form.

9. Vishnu's boar incarnation.

10. Krishna killing the serpent Kaliya.

11. Vishnu with his attributes, a conch, a discus, a mace, and a lotus (*shankha*, *chakra*, *gada*, and *padma*)

12. Goddess Annapurna.

All the sculptures in these galleries were carved later, sometime in the ninth and tenth centuries. They are all of crude workmanship in sharp contrast to the elegant dynamism of those in the main temple and the *Yajna-shala*. They attest to the fact that the rock-cut art was on the decline as structural temples came to be built on a large scale in the ninth and tenth centuries AD.

Cave 17

At some distance from Cave 16 one comes across this cave, which though containing some fine sculptures, has been considerably damaged probably by landslides. The porch is almost destroyed. It was supported by massive pillars with square bases, octagonal shafts and fluted upper part; on the shafts are carved dwarfs at corners. The hall is supported by 12 pillars in three rows dividing it into three transverse bays. The pillars have standing human figures and female bracket figures with attendants that recall those in Cave 21. At the back is the square shrine containing a Shiva *linga*. The door frame is severely plain.

In the northern end of the hall is an image of Ganesha. The god is four-armed and is seen eating sweets with his trunk from a bowl in his lower left hand. On his left is a devotee and in the upper left corner is a flying figure. In his upper left hand is a battle axe and his broken tusk or a radish in the lower right; the upper right hand has a rosary. His bulging belly is secured by a band (*udara-bandha*).

On the opposite wall, the corresponding panel depicts goddess Durga slaying the buffalo demon. She is also four armed, and holds a trident, a shield, and a sword and the fourth is on the mouth of the demon. There are two attendants. In the porch, on the south is Vishnu and in the north is Brahma. The former is much obliterated. The head of the female attendant on his right is missing, but the garland-bearing flying figure in the upper right corner is complete. There was a similar figure on the left which is now totally destroyed. The standing Brahma is four headed (one head at the back) and four armed, and is seen granting a boon. He is flanked by a male on the left and a female on the right; there are flying figures (Vidyadharas) above. Stylistically, the cave can be assigned to the seventh century.

Cave 18

This cave is not much different from Cave 21 in conception as it essentially consists of a hall, a vestibule, and a shrine. The portico has at its base a semi-circular slab (*chandra-shila*). The hall is supported by two square pillars and two pilasters; the pillars have corbelled brackets at the top. The vestibule has square pillars. The shrine, roughly squarish, contains a Shiva *linga*. The cave can be assigned to ca. 700 AD.

Cave 19

This cave is damaged and incomplete, consisting of a squarish shrine with a circumambulatory passage and a pillared hall at the front.

Cave 20A

This plain cave consists of a hall with a verandah at the front. The main door of the hall is flanked by entrances on the sides. The verandah has four square pillars and there is a cell at either end. The pillars of the verandah have two armed corbelled capitals. The vase-and-foliage capitals were intended for the pillars but were not finished. In the court too on either side is a cell each; that in the north contains a *yaksha* image looking like Matanga, associated with the Jaina Tirthankara Mahavir. The cell may be a later addition when the Jaina group at the site was being excavated.

Cave 20B

It is situated close to Cave 21 and is at a slightly higher level. It consists of a roughly squarish shrine with circumambulatory passage all around and elongated chambers in side walls having pillars. There was probably a hall at the front and also portico but these have been ruined beyond recognition. The only surviving feature is the carved doorway of the shrine having Ganga and Yamuna and floral scrolls adorning the jambs; by the side also are Ganga and Yamuna, which are bigger in size, and beyond them are gigantic guardians with a dwarf attendant by their side. Outside, Ganesha and Durga are carved on the north and south walls but are largely destroyed; in front is the pedestal for Nandi.

Cave 21

This was an early cave to be excavated at Ellora and is one of the finest rock-cut temples in India **[Fig 5.23]**. In the court is a pedestal on which is Nandi of Shiva, with carvings on its sides. On either side at the front stand exquisitely carved river goddesses, Ganga on a crocodile on the northern face and Yamuna on a tortoise on the south **[Fig. 5.24]**. Both are colossal images and are so elegantly carved that they stand out as the finest of their class. The alluring curves of the figures are in the Vakataka-Gupta tradition and the cave can therefore be placed in the middle of the sixth century.

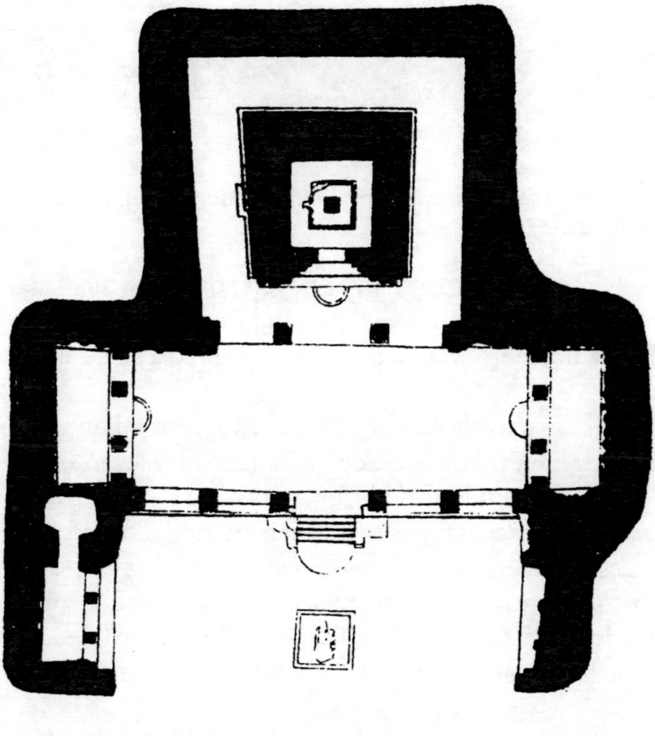

FIg. 5.23. Plan of Cave 21 (Rameshwar).

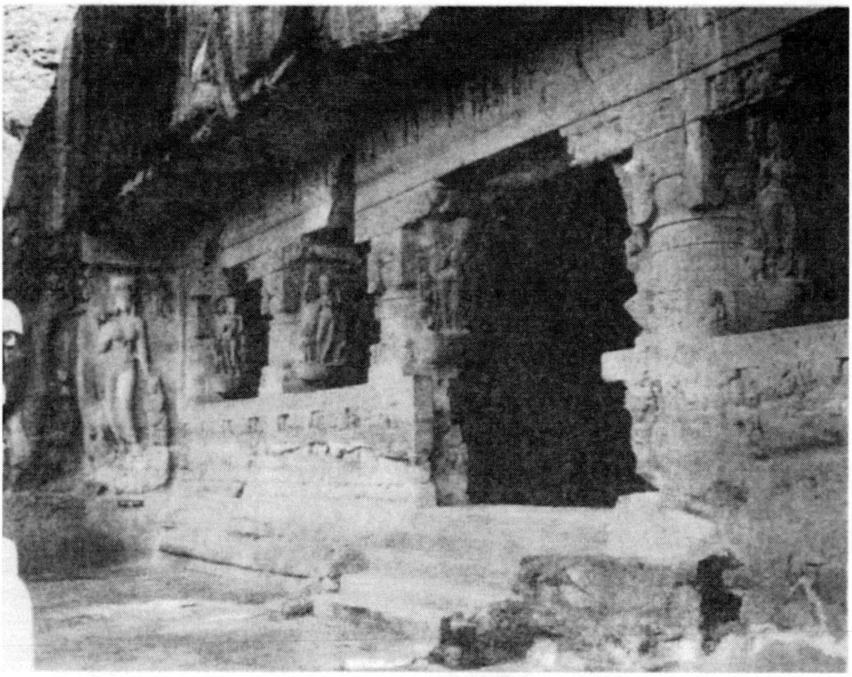

Fig. 5.24. Cave 21 (Rameshwar), front colonnade with entrance, Ganga on the left.

They are seen standing in a slightly flexed posture, which adds to their charm. They have a female attendant each, holding a fly whisk. In the northern wall of the court is carved a small shrine of Ganesha.

The hall has a low wall at the front, with four pillars and two pilasters. They have massive square shafts and very elegantly carved vase-and-foliage capitals. In addition, they have charming damsels (*salabhanjikas*) as bracket figures with their attendant dwarfs leaning against trees. Above them are horned mythical creatures (*shardulas*) topped by a running frieze carved with dainty floral scrolls and frolicking dwarfs. The exterior of the parapet wall is carved with a running frieze of majestic elephants above which are erotic couples (*mithunas*).

The walls of the hall are richly adorned with large sculptured panels. In all probability the hall was originally squarish but became elongated because of the extension of the side chapels which are separated by two pillars having square shafts and cushion capitals.

At the left end of the northern chapel is Kartikeya, the elder son of Shiva who is four armed **[Fig. 5.25]**. He holds a fowl in his left hand and there is a large bird, probably a peacock, his mount, in his right hand. He is flanked by the goat-headed Naigamesha. There are Vidyadharas in the sky.

On the back wall of the northern chapel is a large panel depicting the marriage of Shiva and Parvati (*Kalyana-sundara-murti*). From

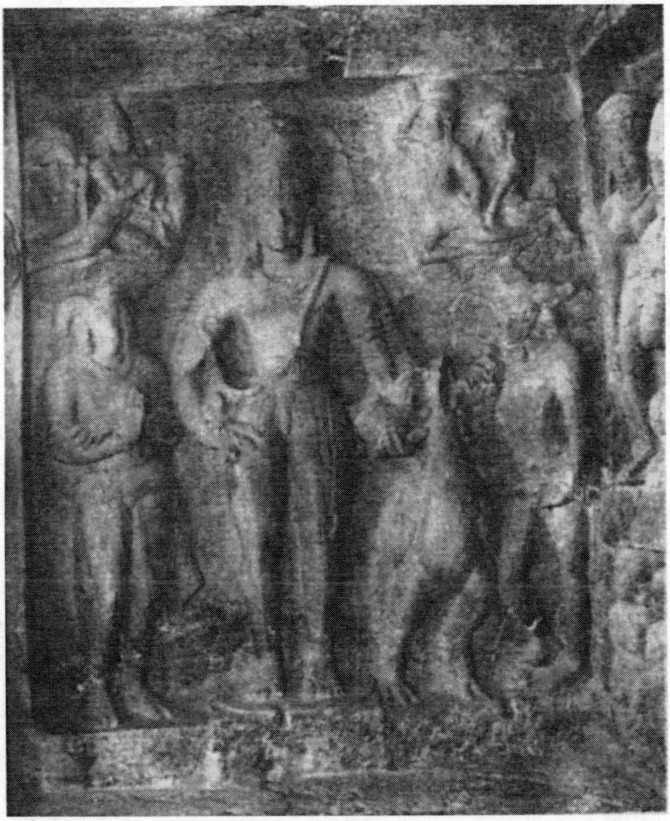

Fig. 5.25. Cave 21 (Rameshwar), northern chapel, west wall, Kartikeya.

the left, there is Brahma, the priest of gods, negotiating with Parvati's father, Himavan, behind whom is Parvati; she wears sparse jewellery. In the next panel we see Shiva holding Parvati's hand. In between them is Ganesha and behind Parvati is the sage Bhringi, an ardent devotee of Shiva. Brahma, the officiating priest, is seen near the sacred fire. Parvati's father, Himavan, is standing between the couple performing *kanya-dana*, the ceremony in which daughter is given to the groom. There are some more figures of which the most important is Vishnu holding a conch (*shankha*).

On the north wall of the northern shrine is a very interesting panel which is the only of its kind at Ellora. It depicts Parvati or Uma, performing a penance, a sort of fire test as the fires before her would indicate. She is shown standing like an ascetic with a rosary in one hand. She performed this penance to get Shiva as her husband. Her female attendants are also present and there are many others; in the frieze below are dwarfs. Shiva, also in the form of a celibate (*brahmachari*) approaches her to test her loyalty. To the right is a tall female figure in front of whom is a youth coming out of crocodile's mouth. He is actually Shiva who is saved by Parvati. These scenes appear to have been inspired by Kalidasa's *Kumarasambhavam* epic. It should have preceded that showing the marriage as Parvati performed the penance for getting Shiva's hand.

On the east end of the northern chamber is goddess Durga slaying the buffalo demon (*Mahisha-mardini Durga*). She has four hands holding a sword, a trident, a shield and the head of the buffalo demon. There is another four-armed figure holding a club, and yet one more with a sword. Above are seen Vidyadharas.

On either side of the shrine are large sculptured panels. On the northern side is Ravana shaking Mount Kailas on which there are Shiva and Parvati with their retinue. Ravana is shown with five heads, one of which looks like that of an animal (boar).

Two pillars separate the squarish shrine from the hall. In front of the pillars are female fly whisk bearers, one each with attendant dwarfs. The pillars have cushion capitals and square abaci which are also carved with figures.

The doorway of the shrine is profusely carved and resembles the late Gupta door frames of the sixth century. The three jambs of the doorway have a pilaster on the central one and that on either side is tastefully decorated with human couples (*mithunas*)—an auspicious symbol—flying figures and mythical creatures, besides chaitya windows. At the base are male and female figures. Inside the shrine is a Shiva *linga* (phallus). The shrine also has a circumambulatory passage. The door frame resembles those in Caves 1 and 4 at Ajanta and hence much time may not have elapsed between them. It also places the date of the cave in the middle of the sixth century.

On the southern side of the hall is shown Shiva and Parvati playing *chausar* (a sort of dice) **[Fig. 5.26]**, Parvati has a few female attendants, one of whom is dressing her hair. In the frieze below are the frolicking *ganas* and Nandi. It seems that Parvati is a little irritated, probably because her lord has cheated her while playing.

In the southern chapel (right side) is a gruesome figure of Kala, the god of death, and his consort, Kali. He has four arms, of which two are broken; one hand holds a curved dagger and in the other is

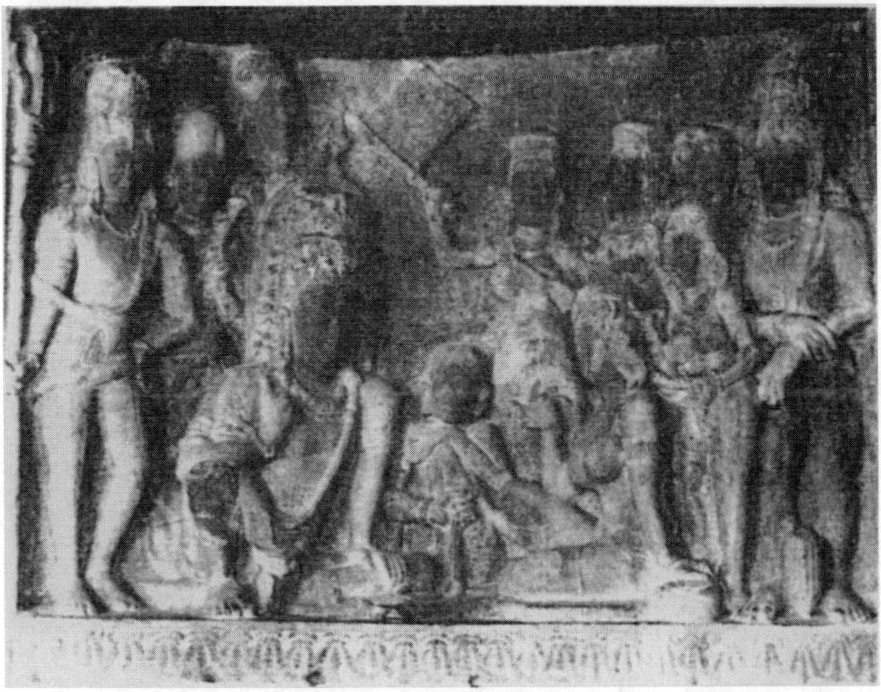

Fig. 5.26. Cave 21 (Rameshwar), Shiva-Parvati playing *chausar*.

a human being. He seems to be dancing with joy. Kali too has a human head in her hand. There is a child and another human figure; a flying Vidyadhara holding a cup is seen above.

On the back wall is Ganesha with seven mother goddesses with their mounts on their seats and Virabhadra. Ganesha who is always present in the *Sapta-matrika* panels, holds in his four hands a battle axe, sweets, (*modaka*), a broken tooth or radish and a rosary (*aksha-mala*). Next to him are the mother goddessess: Chamunda, Indrani, Varahi, Vaishnavi, Kaumari, Maheshwari and Brahmi, each with a child **[Fig. 5.27]**. They are seated with one leg folded and the right one hanging except Brahmi, who is seated in the European fashion. They all wear elaborate jewellery and their coiffures and headdresses are elegant. The last one is Virabhadra.

On the east end is a panel showing Shiva dancing. The god is

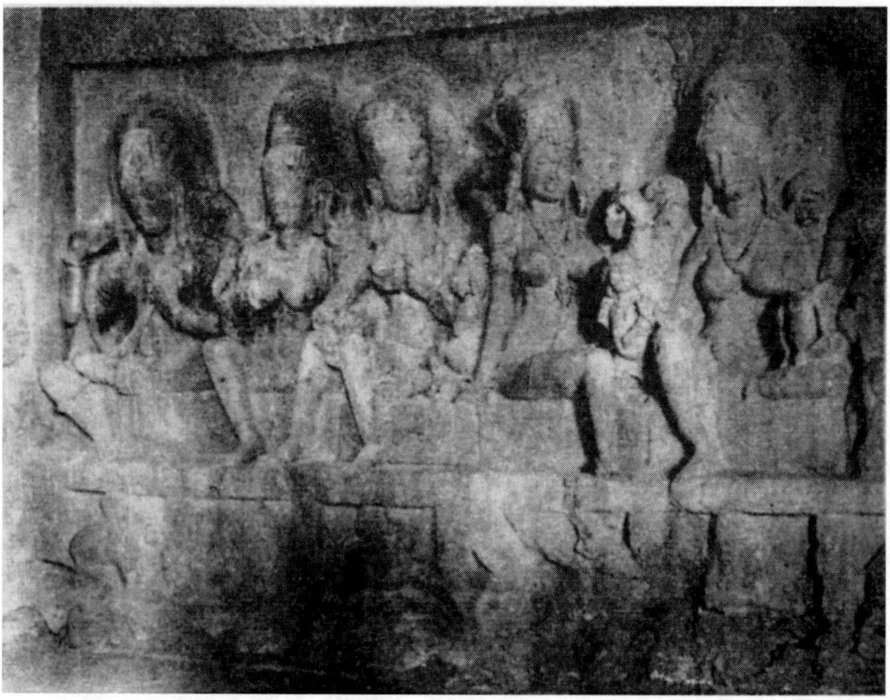

Fig. 5.27. Cave 21 (Rameshwar), part of Sapta-matrika panel, in the southern chapel.

eight-armed, holding various attributes, with Parvati and attendants and musicians. Bhringi is seen between Shiva's legs. Of the eight hands of Shiva, three are broken, yet the figure displays vigour and unbounded energy. Above are the *dikpalas* (guardians of directions) on their mounts.

Cave 22

The cave consists of a shrine, a vestibule, a pillared hall with chambers inside walls and a court at the front in which there is a ruined Nandi pavilion. In the southern wall of the court is a shrine containing the Sapta-matrikas (seven mother goddesses) and Ganesha and Kala. Among the sculptures in the shrine is an image of Ganga.

The cave is locally known as Nilakantha (blue throated), which is one of the names of Shiva.

Cave 23 and 24

These are small shrines.

Cave 25

Locally known as Kumbharwada (Potter's Quarter) or Sureshwar, it is situated at a short distance from Cave 24. It consists of a squarish shrine, a vestibule and a pillared hall with vestibules on sides. The front portion of the hall has been destroyed. At the front was a large court with a shrine in the right wall. The massive pillars are ornamented with bands containing mithunas at the base, the central band has peacocks and the uppermost has lotuses. The vase and foliage capital is elegantly carved and at the top are standing human figures. The brackets too are carved with human figures.

On the ceiling of the antechamber is an image of Surya and hence the name of the cave Sureshwar.

Cave 26

This is known as *Janawasa*, which in the local language—Marathi—means the house given to a bridegroom's party for staying at the time of marriage. The cave is similar in plan to Cave 21. The hall has four pillars at the front and side chambers and a squarish shrine at the back containing a Shiva*linga* with a circumambulatory passage.

Cave 27

This cave is also similar to Cave 26 above but is in a ruined condition.

Cave 28

This cave, consisting of a shrine and a hall, is also completely ruined. The shrine door has guardians and Vidyadharas above. In the western corner of the outer wall is an image of Ambika which seems to be a later addition.

The cave is located on the edge of a ravine where there is a waterfall formed by the stream flowing from the hill. It is a nice scenic spot during the rainy season.

Cave 29

Known as Dumar *lena*, and also as *Sita ki nahani* as it is situated near the waterfall, it is one of the largest caves in western India and it is almost identical on the plan with the main cave at Elephanta near Mumbai **[Fig. 5.28]**. A low flight of steps with lions and small elephants under their paws at the entrance leads to the great hall **[Fig. 5.29]** The plan resembles a cross with the main shrine at the back. The hall is supported by four rows of four pillars, each which divide it into five aisles besides two each in the side vestibules. The pillars are massive with square shafts and cushion capitals.

The entire cave is adorned with large sculptured panels containing gigantic figures. Starting from the entrance, on the right wall (south) is Ravana shaking Mount Kailas with his eight hands, and on the left (north) on the opposite wall is Andhakasura-*vadha-murti* Shiva. The god is eight armed and holds a sword, a bowl, a snake and has a stretched elephant hide over his head. His sword is thrust in the demon's body. He looks ferocious with his eyes

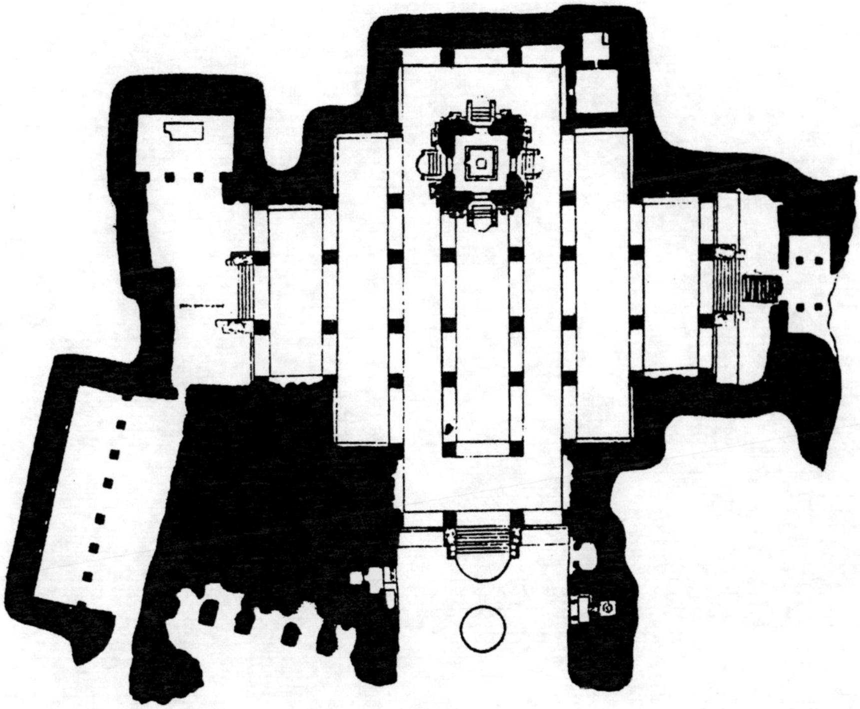

FIg. 5.28. Plan of Cave 29 (Dumar Lena).

bulging out. Parvati stands to his left. The figures are gigantic but look rather disproportionate and earthbound.

On the west wall of the south verandah are Shiva and Parvati playing chausar with Nandi and the frolicking dwarfs in the lower band. Vishnu and Brahma are also seen in this panel on the left and right. There is a large pit cut into the floor in the south verandah, which may have been used for some sacrifice. On the eastern wall of this verandah is shown the marriage of Shiva and Parvati **[Fig. 5.30]**. The entire composition is similar to that in the preceding caves, the only difference is that the panel being very large, the figures are outsize. Outside the pilaster, to the south of this is a colossal image of a goddess with four ascetics above and three females below; a bird pulls at her mantle. She may have been intended as Ganga but

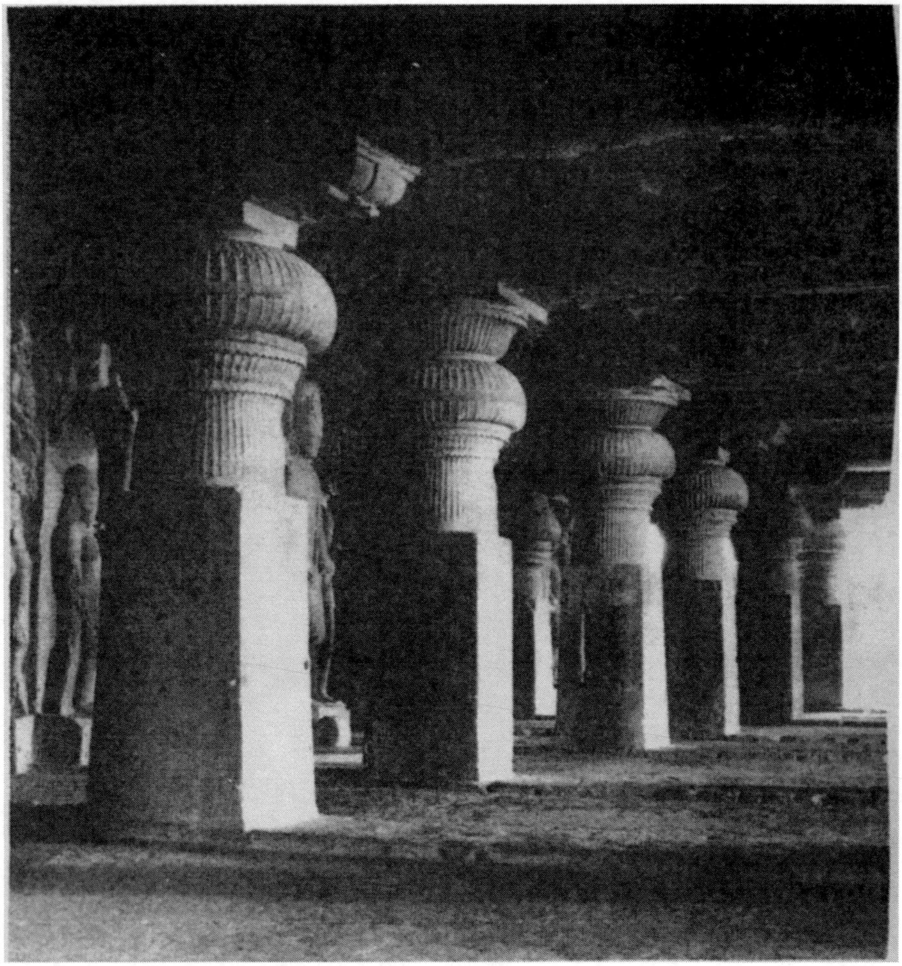

FIg. 5.29. Cave 29 (Dumar Lena), interior.

her mount is not carved. The corresponding figure outside the western portico is that of Yamuna. On the south of this verandah are a few steps leading to the waterfall and a pool below. In the corresponding verandah on the north, on the east wall, is a huge image of Lakulisha, sitting on a lotus and holding a club in his left hand; the lotus is supported by cobra kings with two worshippers

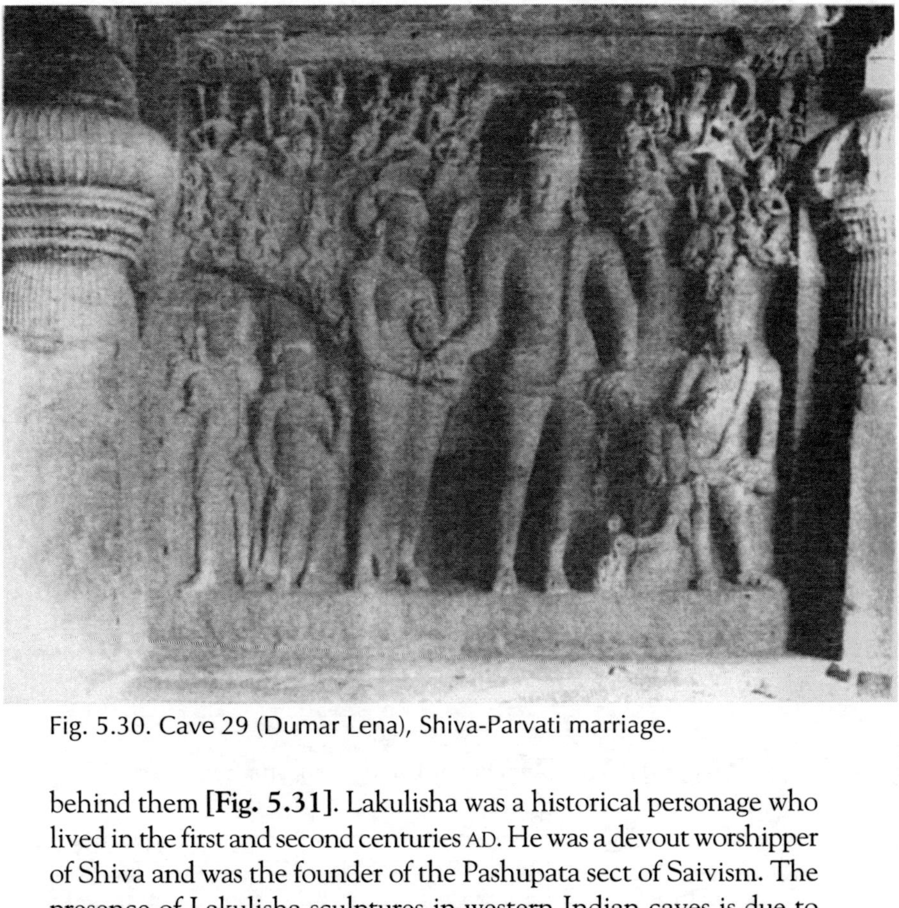

Fig. 5.30. Cave 29 (Dumar Lena), Shiva-Parvati marriage.

behind them **[Fig. 5.31]**. Lakulisha was a historical personage who lived in the first and second centuries AD. He was a devout worshipper of Shiva and was the founder of the Pashupata sect of Saivism. The presence of Lakulisha sculptures in western Indian caves is due to the Kalachuri kings who were ruling in western India in the fifth and sixth centuries. They were the followers of the Pashupata cult.

On the opposite (east) wall of the northern verandah is Shiva dancing the tandav. To the left of Shiva is Parvati and to his right are Nandi (Shiva's bull) and musicians. Above, to the left are Brahma on a lotus, Varuna on a crocodile, Vayu on a stag, and Yama on a buffalo. On the right we see Indra on an elephant, Agni on a ram and Vishnu on an eagle. These are the dikpalas. On the east wall, outside is Yamuna on a tortoise. She has a single female attendant and there are Vidyadharas in the sky.

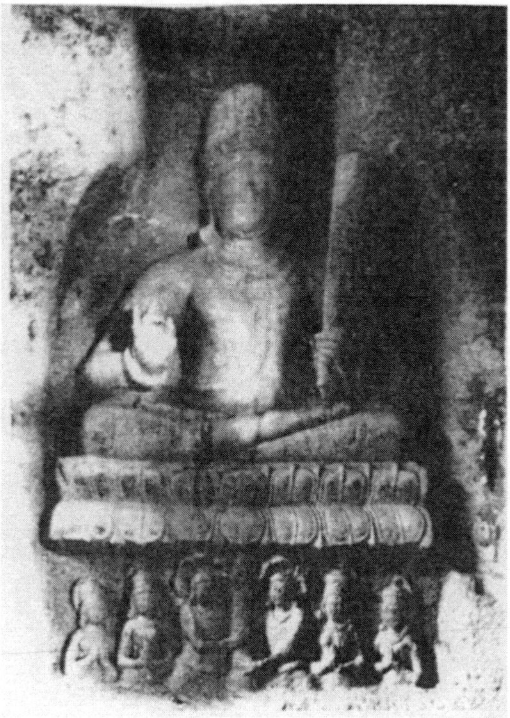

Fig. 5.31. Cave 29 (Dumar Lena), Lakulisha.

The shrine is not carved in the back wall but is independent and can be circumambulated **[Fig. 5.32]**. It is square in plan and contains a Shiva *linga*. It has four entrances, one on each side with a flight of steps. There are huge guardians on the door one each on either side, with a female attendant. Although it is a very large cave with gigantic sculptures, they are not as elegant as those in the Rameshwar (Cave 21) or at Elephanta, which are artistically superior. The figures are corpulent and stumpy with disproportionate limbs. The spiritual experience too is missing. However, on stylistic grounds, the cave can be dated to the seventh century.

Ganesha Lena

Locally known as Ganesha Lena, this group is located above Cave 29, at a distance of about 100 m. These are small shrines which may

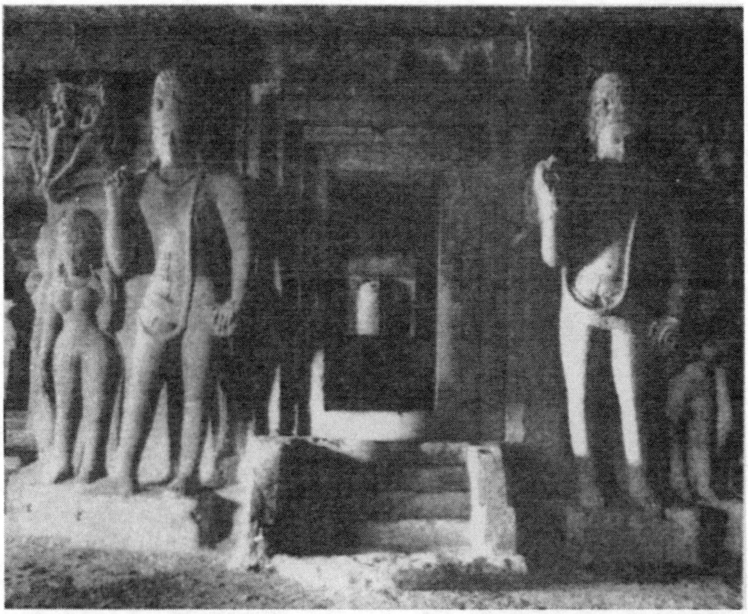

FIg. 5.32. Cave 29 (Dumar Lena), shrine in the hall.

be of a much later date. Among them is one which consists of a hall with two pillars and a shrine in the back wall. The cave is noteworthy for its paintings on walls, one of which depicts the *Lingodbhava-murti Shiva*, wherein Shiva emerges out of a phallus and Brahma and Vishnu are flanking him. This panel is executed on the eastern side of the ceiling, whereas in the centre the churning of the ocean (*samudra-manthana*) is depicted.

In another group there are images of Ganesha and Shiva as Trimurti. The Yogeshwari group is located still higher up. They also contain figures of Shiva as Trimurti. All these caves are not very artistic and can be assigned on stylistic grounds to the twelfth century.

SIX

Jaina Caves

The Jaina group at Ellora, containing only five caves, is situated in the northern part of the hill beyond Cave 29, the last Hindu cave. The founder of Jainism, Mahavira (599 BC–527 BC) was a senior contemporary of Buddha. He was one of the 24 *Tirthankaras*, among whom Parshvanath (23rd *Tirthankara*), who lived 350 years before Mahavira, is also said to be a historical personage. Of the 24 *Tirthankaras*, the first 22 are supposed to be mythical. Rishabha or Adinath and Parshvanath are the most important of the Tirthankaras, and so also is Shantinath to a lesser extent. But Mahavira can be said to be the true founder of Jainism although he was the last *Tirthankara*. He was born of Brahmin parents, Rishabhadatta and Devananda, at Vaishali, in present-day Bihar. He was brought up with great care and was well-trained in arts and sciences. He was married to Yashoda and had a daughter by her. When he lost his parents at the age of 28, he decided to renounce the world, left his family, distributed his property among the poor, became an ascetic and practised austerities. After thirteen years of penance, he saw the light and became an *arhat*—all knowing—and a *Jina*, a conqueror. He began to preach and those who accepted his teachings came to be known as Jainas. He was then recognised as a great hero, 'Mahavira'.

The next 30 years of his life he spent in preaching and gained many adherents to Jainism.

Jainism became quite popular among trading communities and was patronised by them. A majority of the Jainas today are merchants and traders, mostly from Western India. Buddhism spread beyond India but finally vanished from the land of its origin, but Jainism, which did not go out of the country, is still a flourishing religion in India.

The Jaina caves at Ellora belong to the ninth and tenth centuries. They all belong to the Digambara (sky-clad) sect and the figures are not shown wearing any clothes. The other sect, Shvetambara—those who wear white garments—is not represented at Ellora.

The sculptural representation in Ellora of the Jaina caves is quite limited and the same images are repeated over and over again. They include Parshvanath, Mahavira, Gomateshvara, the *Yaksha* Matanga and *Yakshi* Siddhayika with Chakreshvari occurring rarely. Gomateshvara is the same as Bahubali in north India. He was the second son of Rishabhanath, a *jina*, a ruler of Taxila. Although he was victorious in his conflict with Bharat, his step brother, he realised the futility of it all and renounced the world for attaining salvation. He became an ascetic and performed rigorous austerities by standing in an erect posture (*kayostsarga mudra*) for a year. This is how he is represented in art with creepers, snakes, and scorpions around him. He is flanked by two *jinas* and Bharat. The best example is in the western *mandapa* of Cave 32.

The Jaina group at Ellora was probably excavated during the reign of the Rashtrakuta king Amoghavarsha (819–81) who was a great patron of Jainism and the work may have continued later as an inscription in Cave 32 shows.

Cave 30

There are five Jaina caves at Ellora of which the first (30) is known as Chhotah Kailas (small Kailas) as it resembles the great Kailas (16) but is much smaller. It resembles a temple in the Dravidian style of South India, an important feature of which is the tower (*shikhara*) in receding tiers. It consists of a squarish hall, supported by 16 pillars and a shrine at the back. The portico is squarish. The entire temple is scooped out of a solid block of rock which is separated from the surrounding hill as in the case of Kailas. A noteworthy aspect of this temple is that the upper parts are finished whereas the lower ones are unfinished indicating that in cave architecture work started from the top.

The gopura is rather inartistic. On its side walls, on the interior are carved Tirthankaras but more interesting is the twelve-armed Chakreshvari, the yakshi of Rishabhanath. She holds a lotus, a discus, a conch, a mace and even a sword, and wears elaborate jewellery. Her mount, an eagle, is seen below her seat. On the portico are two dancing figures of yaksha Sourandhendra, above whom is a small image of Mahavira with his attendants. There is another six-armed yaksha on the left of the portico. A loose sculpture of a female in the portico is dated Saka 1169 (1247 AD), which evidently is much later than its date. There are traces of paintings on the ceiling. In the hall are several images of Tirthankaras. They are also carved on the entrance gateway.

Cave 31

This small cave, though unfinished, consists of a four-pillared hall and a shrine. On the left wall of the hall is an exquisite Parshvanath above whom are seven hoods of the cobra king Dharanendra. On the left is Mahavira. On the back wall is yaksha Matanga on an elephant having foliage at his back and flanked by attendants. His consort Siddhayika is also seen on the right of the shrine door. On the right wall of the hall is Gomateshvara, standing erect in the *kayotsarga* posture. Inside the shrine is Mahavira.

Cave 32

The two most complete and ornate caves in the Jaina group are the Indra Sabha (32) and the Jagannath Sabha (33). Cave 32 got the appellation Indra Sabha (Indra's court) probably because it is highly ornate and also because of the sculpture of Matanga on an elephant, which was wrongly identified as that of Indra. It is a double-storied cave with one more shrine in its court **[Fig. 6.1]**. The court,

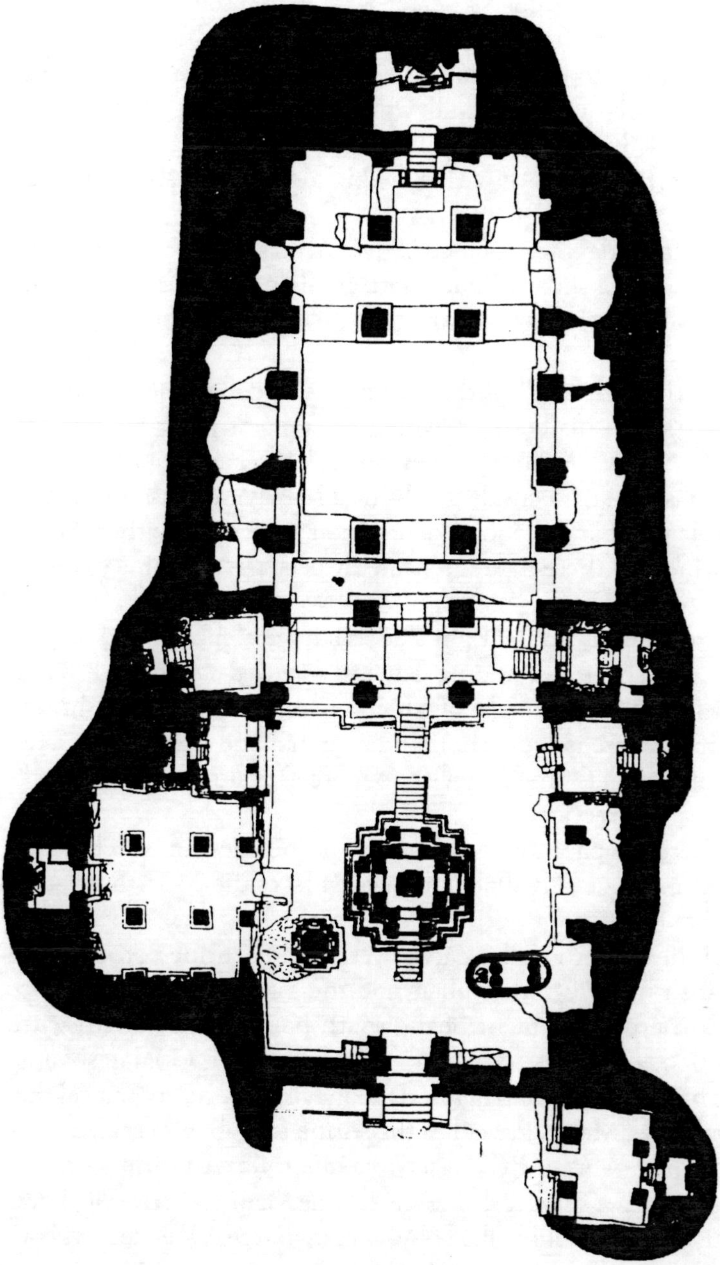

Fig. 6.1. Plan of Cave 32 (Indra-sabha), ground floor.

which is entered through a screen wall facing south, has a small shrine outside in the western (left) wall supported by four pillars, two at the front and two inside. The walls are sculptured with images of Parshvanath on the left wall, whose distinguishing attribute is a seven-hooded cobra; an umbrella over his head is held by a female attendant **[Fig. 6.2]**. Above her is a buffalo rider. Parshvanath was Mahavira's senior and his parents are said to have been his followers. On his left is a devotee couple. Above them is a demon (Kamatha) riding what looks like a lion. There are flying Vidyadharas in the sky and below in the left hand corner are two female cobras in human form.

On the right wall of the shrine is a nude Gomateshvara or Bahubali, with his body entwined in creepers **[Fig. 6.3]**. He is attended by devotees and females; on his left is Parshvanath and on the right is Mahavira. Inside the shrine is Mahavira. Yaksha Matanga on an elephant and Siddhayika on a lion are seen on either side of the shrine. All these figures repeatedly occur in the Jaina caves at Ellora.

In the court, on the right side, is a huge elephant and on the left is a massive free-standing flag post (*dhavaja-stambha*). It has a squarish base on each face of which is carved a miniature shrine. The shaft above is squarish, then octagonal and then fluted. The cushion capital is crowned with four ascetics sitting back to back facing each direction.

There is a pavilion in the centre of the court in which is enshrined an image of Rishabhanath, the first of the 24 Tirthankaras, or Mahavira.

In the western wall is carved yet another shrine consisting of a squarish hall with four pillars and the sanctum at the back. In the central compartment of the south hall is Parshvanath with cobra hoods over his head and in the opposite is Gomateshvara. In the back wall are Matanga and Siddhayika, the attendant yaksha and yakshi of Mahavira and in the shrine is Mahavira seated on a lion throne; over his head is a triple umbrella. Adjoining on the north is another smaller shrine containing Matanga on an elephant and his consort Siddhayika below a mango tree. Over this and on the opposite side are similar shrines.

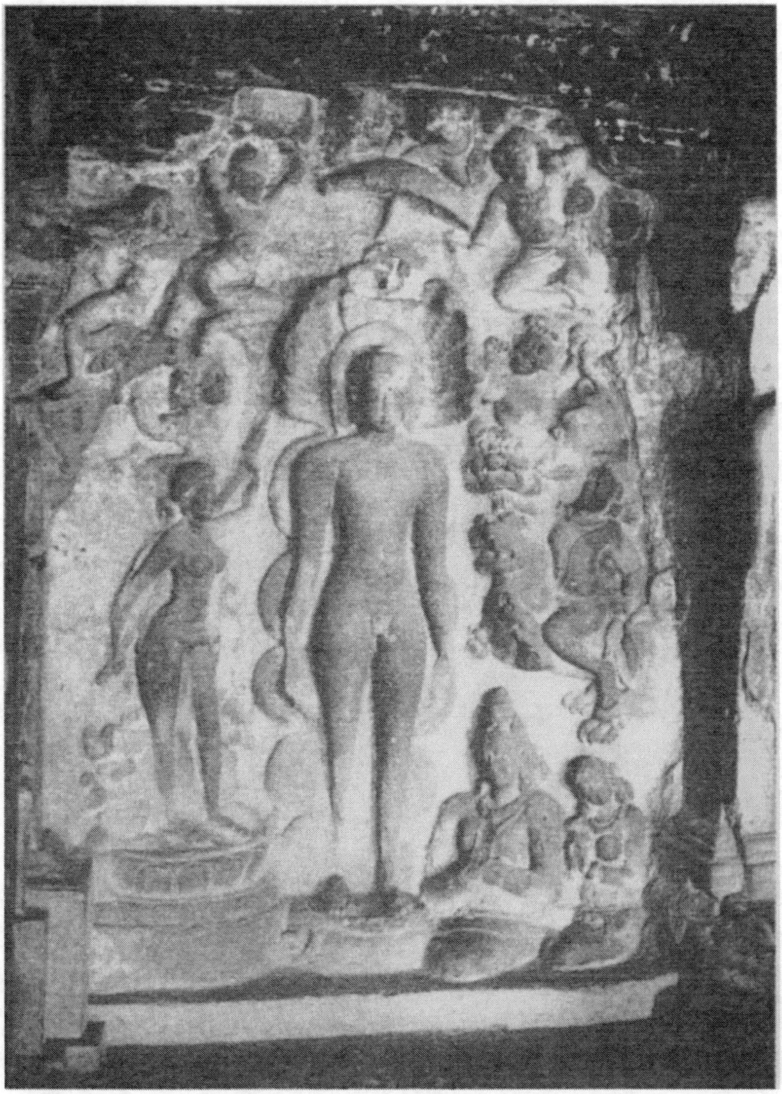

Fig. 6.2. Cave 32 (Indra-sabha), Parshvanath.

The main structure is double-storied. The ground floor consists of a hall with a double verandah. It is supported by twelve squarish pillars, some of which are unfinished. In the front verandah, on the pilasters are two huge images of Shantinath, the 16th tirthankara.

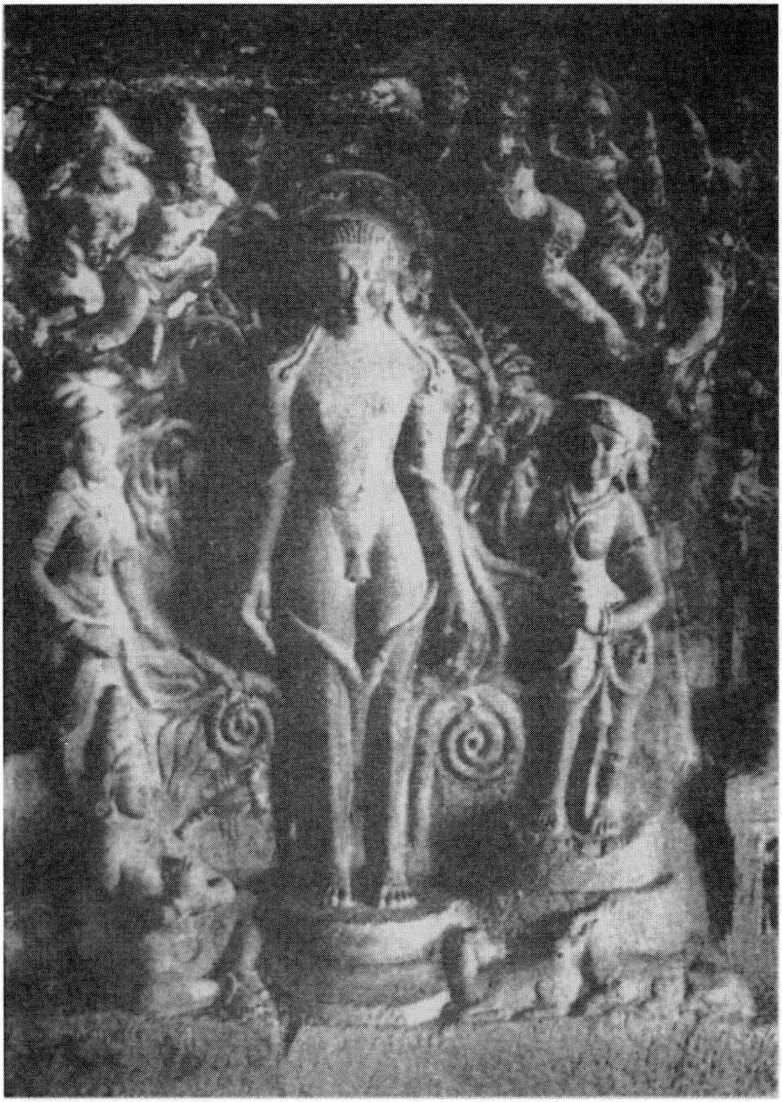

Fig. 6.3. Cave 32 (Indra-sabha), Gomateshvara or Bahubali, in the lower hall, north wall.

According to the inscription engraved underneath, it was the gift of one Sohila, a brahmachari. Palaeographically, it can be assigned to the ninth century. Behind this is another image of a Tirthankara on the pilaster below which is an inscription recording that it was a gift of Nagavarmma. At the left end of the verandah is another shrine with Parshvanath on the left wall, Gomateshvara on the right wall and Mahavira in the shrine guarded by Matanga and Siddhayika.

Upper Floor

A flight of stairs in the eastern end of the verandah leads to the upper floor **[Fig. 6.4]** It consists of a large, squarish hall, supported by 12 pillars disposed in such a manner that an aisle is formed along the sides. The pillars are very elegantly carved, some with vase-and-foliage motif crowned by cushion capitals. They resemble those in the Lankeshwar cave. Some have moulded bases and sixteen-

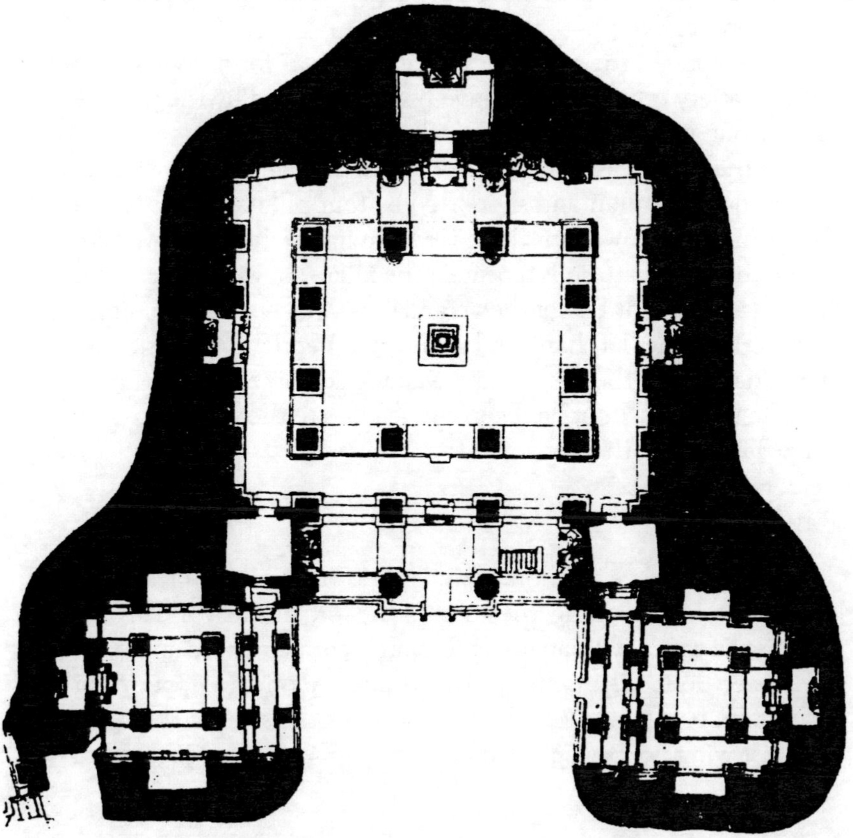

Fig. 6.4. Plan of Cave 32 (Indra-sabha), upper floor.

sided shafts with cushion capitals and decorative bands carved with charming floral patterns. Huge figures of Matanga and Siddhayika under banana and mango trees respectively have been carved in the verandah at opposite ends **[Fig. 6.5]**. On the side walls are images of Tirthankaras and Jinas. In the centre of each wall is a shrine containing a huge Jina and on the shrine door are Parshvanath and Gomateshvara. On the pilasters flanking the shrines are guardians. The shrine door is profusely carved with a variety of motifs such as Jinas, human figures, and flying Vidyadharas, besides two pilasters with cushion capitals. In the centre of the hall was the *sarvato-bhadra-pratima*, which has four images on four sides which, however, is destroyed. Exactly above this in the centre of the ceiling is carved a huge lotus flower. The holes in the corners of the hall are probably for suspending lamps.

It is noteworthy that the entire cave was formerly painted with a variety of motifs that have been blackened by the passage of time but are now being chemically cleaned.

In the south-eastern corner of the upper hall are two smaller caves, square in plan and supported by four pillars and having a shrine in the back wall in which is Mahavira. In the south-western shrine the same pattern is repeated; the pillars, however, are better carved. In the right end of the verandah is Chakreshvari holding a manuscript in her left hand and a chakra in her right. Opposite her is Siddhayika. At the other end is Matanga on an elephant.

On the left, a door has been cut, leading to the second floor of Cave 33, Jagannath Sabha.

Cave 33

This is the last cave at Ellora which is known locally as Jagannath Sabha, literally meaning 'the court of the lord of the world'. It is a complex of caves, with an upper floor. It is convenient to approach the upper floor first as the visitor is already on the upper floor of Indra Sabha (Cave 32). In the corner of the smaller shrine in the west wing is a passage leading to the upper floor of Jagannath Sabha.

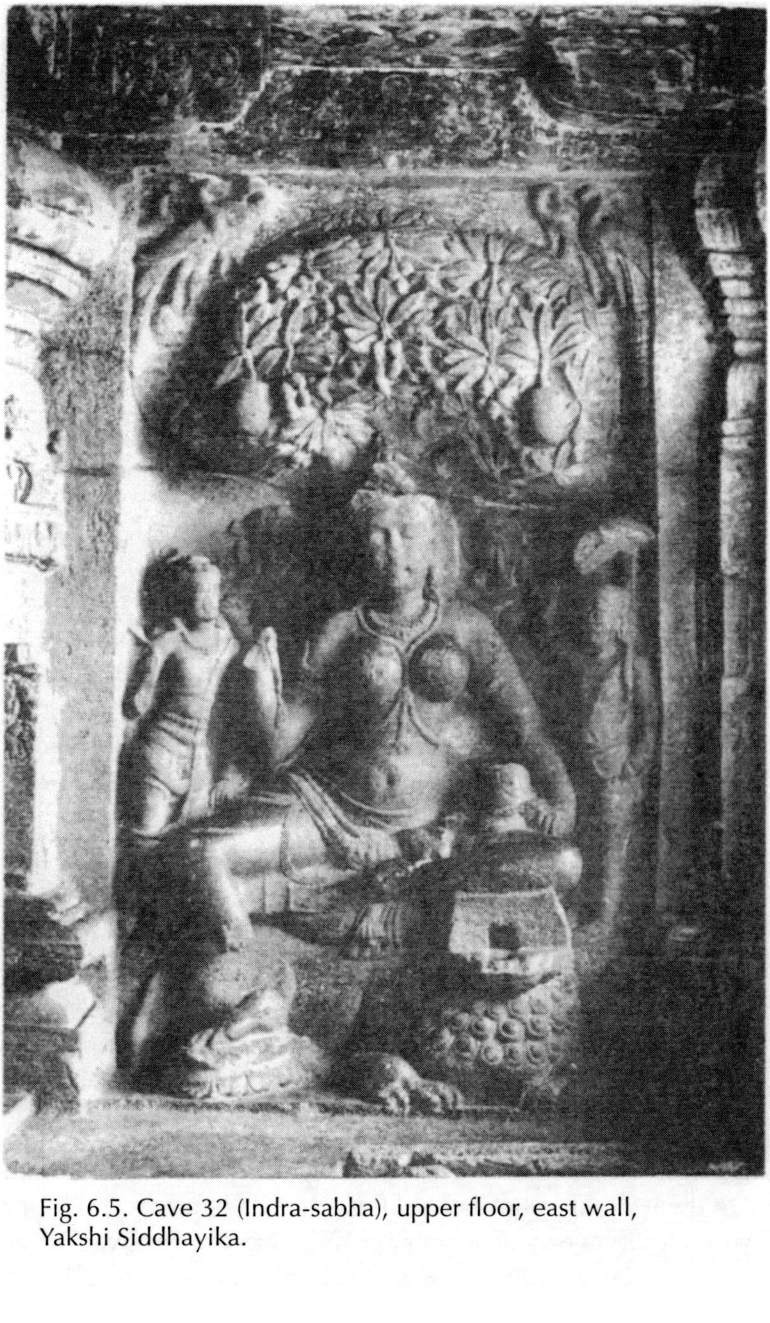

Fig. 6.5. Cave 32 (Indra-sabha), upper floor, east wall, Yakshi Siddhayika.

Upper Floor

The upper floor is similar to that of Cave 32. It consists of a shrine and a huge pillared hall on the walls of which are carved numerous images of Mahavira and Parshvanath. Besides, there are paintings on the ceiling and also on the walls, wherever space was available. The paintings generally comprise geometric patterns and *Jinas* with their devotees. They are now being chemically cleaned.

On either side of the shrine in the back wall are nude guardians with Matanga on an elephant on the left and Siddayika on a lion on the right. On the intricately-carved door frame there are Ganga and Yamuna on either side and on the door jambs are 24 Jaina Tirthankaras.

Ground Floor

From the south-western corner of the upper floor one can descend to the ground floor, where the same pattern is repeated. On the west is a small cave consisting of a double-verandah with pillars, a squarish hall with four pillars and a shrine in the back wall joined to it by a vestibule. Matanga and Siddhayika are in the verandah, Parshvanath is in the left wall and Gomateshvar in the right side shrine whereas in the main shrine is Mahavira. There were inscriptions on pillars which are now mostly worn; a few letters that have survived suggest that the cave may have been built at around the ninth century.

Cave 34

This small cave can be approached through an opening on the left side of Cave 33. There are no sculptures in the verandah but in the hall on either side of the shrine of Mahavira, there are Matanga and Siddhayika, which are among the finest of their class. On the side walls are Parshvanath and Gomateshvara.

Parshvanath Cave

On the west, at some distance from the last Jaina cave, is located yet another cave that contains a colossal image of Parshvanath, and hence its name. But the cave is now hidden in a structure that was built in the last century by a Jain merchant with a view to protecting the image from sun and rain. The image, shown seated on a lion seat (*simhasana*), is about 3 m in height and has seven cobra hoods over his head. He is flanked by devotees. An inscription on the seat mentions that the image way gifted by one Chakreshvara in Saka 1156 (i.e. 1234 AD).

There are some more Jaina caves nearby but all are completely ruined.

Ghrishneshvar Temple

The temple, located in the village Verul (Ellora), at some distance from the caves is ascribed to Ahilyadevi (1765–95), a Holkar prince of Indore. It is a fine architectural specimen with some influence of Mughal style, which is discernable in the turrets, which are the copies of ribbed domes. The shikhara is built in receding tires and the crowning dome rises from petals. Incidentally, it may be mentioned that Verul was the ancestral home of Maloji Bhosale, the grandfather of Shivaji.

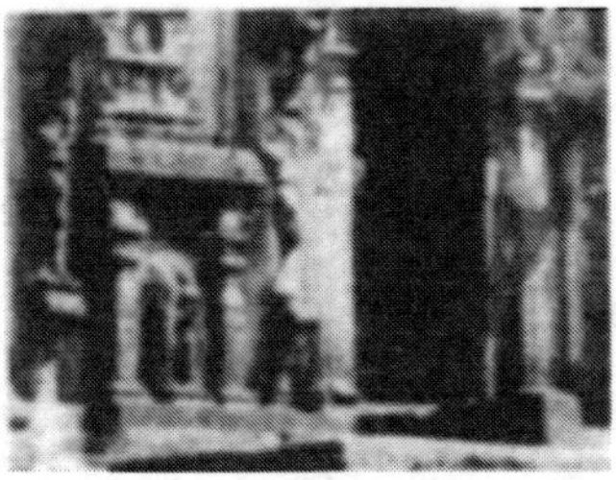

Practical Information

The rock-cut temples at Ellora (20° 21° N, 75°10'E) are situated 27 km north-east of Aurangabad in Maharashtra **[Fig. 1]**. The group contains 34 caves carved in a low hill called the Charanadri, about 1.5 km west of Verul, the anglicised form of which is Ellora. Aurangabad is well connected by road, rail, and air. Flights from New Delhi and Mumbai to Aurangabad are conveniently scheduled and so are rail connections from Mumbai, Pune, and Hyderabad. By road, Aurangabad is 225 km from Pune and 480 km from Mumbai. There are a number of good hotels at Aurangabad, from modest ones to five star establishments as also government lodges near the railway station. One can reach Ellora from Aurangabad by bus or taxi, both of which are available. The State Government's tourist office is located near the railway station and the Government of India tourist office, on Station Road.

Aurangabad to Ellora is a short and pleasant journey with hills on the north and short passes on way. Midway at 15 km stands the impregnable fort of Daulatabad, which was the capital of the Yadavas who ruled over the Deccan from 1060 to 1296 AD. After Daulatabad, the road crosses a short pass. Just before the caves is the village of

Khuldabad, where one can visit the tomb of Shaikh Zainuddin, a great Muslim saint revered by Mughal emperor Aurangzeb (1658–1707). Even though Aurangzeb died at Ahmednagar, 103 km south of Aurangabad, his body was sent to Khuldabad, where his tomb is located next to that of the saint. It is a modest structure that one may visit if one has time. Close to the caves is a scenic pass which decends into Ellora. One can get down here and start seeing the caves. Cave 1 is located just by the road.

Winter (November to February) is the best season to visit Ellora. The monsoon months (June to September) are also enjoyable as the weather is pleasant and there is green everywhere.

A majority of tourists spend only a day at Ellora. Since it is impossible to see all the caves, it is suggested that one should see caves 5, 10, 11, 12, 14, 15, 16, 21, 29, 32, 33, 34 only. They all can be covered in one day.

Aurangabad itself is an important tourist centre. It was of great importance in the medieval period when it was the headquarters of the Mughal viceroy in the Deccan. Its earlier name was '*Khirki*', meaning 'window', thereby implying that it was the window over the Deccan. It was named Aurangabad after the Mughal emperor Aurangzeb, who was viceroy here from 1653–8.

Of the places of tourist interest in the city, the most important is Bibi-ka-Maqbara in Begampura suburb. It contains the tomb of Aurangzeb's wife Begam Rabia Durrani, built between 1650 and 1657. It is a copy of the Taj Mahal at Agra, but is built with brick and plastered with lime.

Another monument is the medieval water mill (*pan-chakki*) for grinding grain, in the western part of the town. It was built around 1695. For the mill, water was brought through an underground conduit from the river Harsul, and was made to fall in the pan-chakki cistern from some height in order to generate necessary power to drive the mill.

But much older and interesting are the three groups of rock-cut caves in the hills behind the Bibi-ka-Maqbara. The first two groups are Buddhist, containing exquisite sculptures of the sixth century AD. The third group consists of one cave only which, however, is unfinished.

There are two historical museums in the city, one in the university and the other in Soneri Mahal, which belongs to the state government. They mostly contain medieval artifacts, coins, and documents.

Paithan, ancient Pratishthan, is situated 60 km south of Aurangabad, on the northern bank of the Godavari. It was the capital of the Satavahanas from the second century BC to the second century AD and earlier still the capital of the Ashmaka republic in the sixth century BC. It was of great religious importance and also an educational centre. It was the home town of the great Marathi saint Eknath. Presently, Paithan is known for its brocaded silk (*paithani*), in the weaving of which golden thread is used.

About 100 km north of Aurangabad are situated the world famous Ajanta caves (ca. second century BC–fifth century AD) known for the paintings on their walls. Ajanta is also a world heritage site.

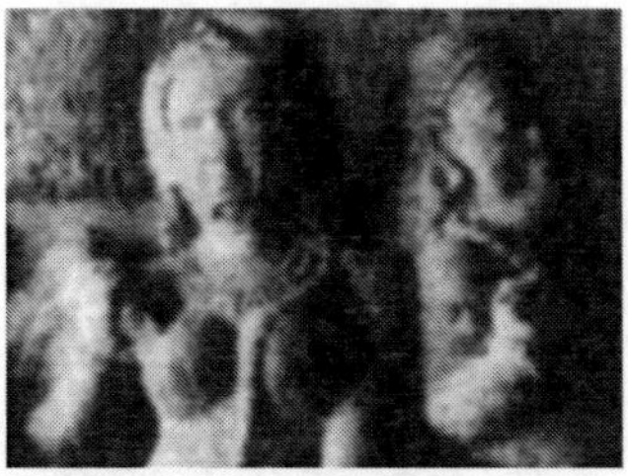

Glossary

Abhaya-mudra	:	Attitude granting protection
ajina	:	deer skin
aksha-mala	:	rosary
antarala	:	vestibule
apsidal	:	circular termination of a structure
ashta-maha-bhayas	:	eight great dangers
ashva-medha	:	horse sacrifice
avatara	:	incarnation
ayudha-purusha	:	personification of a weapon
Bhumi-sparsha-mudra	:	attitude of touching the earth with right hand
Bodhisattva	:	a divinity who has not yet reached Buddhahood
Brahmachari	:	celibate
Buddha	:	The Enlightened One
Capital	:	crowning member of a pillar
cell	:	monk's room
chaitya	:	stupa
chaitya-griha	:	hall containing a stupa
chakra	:	discus

chausar	:	game of dice
chintamani jewel	:	wish-fulfilling jewel
Damaru	:	a small hour-glass shaped drum
dashavatara	:	ten incarnations of Vishnu
dharma	:	religion, righteousness
dharma-chakra-pravartana-mudra	:	attitude of turning the Wheel of Law
dhyana	:	meditation
dhwaja-stambha	:	flag post or pillar
Digambara	:	a Jaina sect, members of which were naked or 'sky-clad'
dikpala	:	guardian of direction
dwarapala	:	door-keeper
Gada	:	mace
gana	:	dwarf
garbha-griha	:	sanctum sanctorum
garuda	:	eagle
ghata	:	vase
ghata-pallava	:	vase and foliage
gopuram	:	entrance gateway of a temple
gotra	:	family
Harmika	:	a squarish box-life member crowning a stupa
Hinayana	:	a Buddhist sect, members of which believed in symbolic worship of Buddha
jata-mukuta	:	matted locks
Jina	:	conqueror
Jyotir-linga	:	column of fire in the form of phallus
Kalasha	:	finial
kamandalu	:	a bowl-like receptacle made of cut gourd
kapala	:	skull
Kayotsarga-mudra	:	attitude of standing erect with hands hanging down
Kirti-mukha	:	lion or demon-like head
Laguda	:	wooden club

lenalene	:	rock-cut cave
lingam	:	phallus
Lokapala	:	guardian deity of direction
Maha-jana-pada	:	great republic
maha-purusha-lakshana	:	marks of great men
Mahayana	:	a Buddhist sect, members of which worshipped Buddha in human form
makara	:	crocodile
makara-torana	:	arch with crocodile heads at terminals
mandapa	:	hall
mithuna	:	couple
modaka	:	sweets
mudra	:	attitude
mukha-mandapa	:	entrance porch
mukuta	:	crown
Naga	:	cobra
Nandi	:	Shiva's bull (his mount)
nirvana	:	Buddha's death
Padma	:	lotus
padmasana	:	lotus seat, seated posture in which soles of feet touch each other
panchayatana	:	a temple with five subsidiary shrines
parashu	:	battle axe
Patala	:	nether world
prabha-valaya	:	halo
pradakshina-patha	:	circumambulatory path
pralamba-padasana	:	sitting with legs hanging down
pralaya	:	doomsday
Sabha-mandapa	:	congregation hall
samudra-manthana	:	churning of the ocean
sangha	:	monastic order
sanghati	:	robe of a Buddhist monk
sarvato-bhadra-pratima	:	Jina images on four sides of a pillar or block
shakti	:	female consort

shala-bhanjika	:	young damsel clinging to a tree
shardula	:	mythical lion-like animal
shesha	:	the great serpent on which Vishnu reclines
shikhara	:	spire, tower
Shvetambara	:	a Jaina sect, members of which wore only white garments
simhasana	:	lion seat
stupa	:	originally a funeral mound or tumulus, but later enshrining relics of Buddha or some venerable monk, it consists of a cylindrical base with a domical top
stupi	:	small domical member crowning a temple tower
Tirtha	:	a sacred place
Tirthankara	:	one of the twenty four founders of Jainism
triratna	:	three jewels of Buddhism—Buddha, dharma and sangha
trishula	:	trident
Udarabandha	:	belly hand
urna	:	small protrusion between eyebrows, a mark of great men
ushnisha	:	protrusion on the head, a mark of great men
Vajra	:	thunderbolt
vana	:	forest
vassa-vasa	:	abode during rainy season
Vidyadhara	:	a class of semi-divine creatures
vihara	:	residence for monks
vina	:	lute, a stringed instrument
vyala	:	mythical animal
Yajna	:	sacrifice
yajna-shala	:	hall of sacrifice
yajnopavita	:	sacred thread
yaksha	:	semi-divine male
yakshi	:	semi-divine female

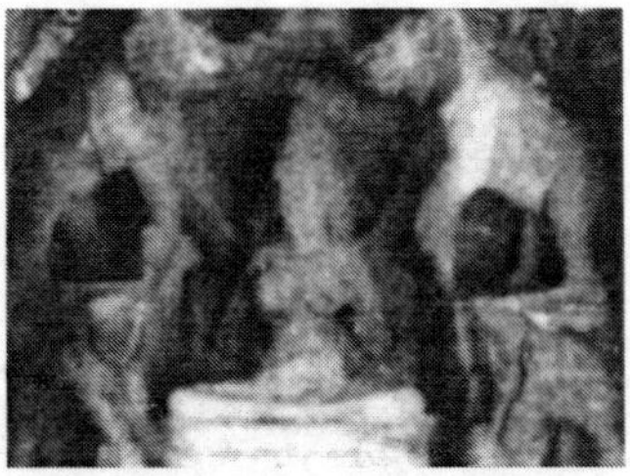

Bibliography

Brown, Percy, *Indian Architecture, Vol. I, Buddhist and Hindu*, Bombay, 1971.

Burgess, James, *Report on the Buddhist Cave Temples and Their Inscriptions*, Archaeological Survey of Western India, Vol. IV, London, 1883.

Burgess, James, *Report on the Ellora Cave Temples and the Brahmanical and Jaina Caves in Western India*, Archaeological Survey of Western India, Vol. V, London, 1883.

Burgess, James and Indraji, Bhagwanlal, *Inscriptions from the Cave Temples of India*, Bombay, 1881.

Dhavalikar, M.K., *Kailas–Ellora: Masterpieces of Rashtrakuta Art*, Bombay, 1983.

Fergusson, James and Burgess, James, *Cave Temples of India*, London, 1880.

Gupte, R.S. and Mahajan, B.D., *Ajanta, Ellora and Aurangabad Caves*, Bombay, 1962.

Parimoo, Ratan *et al.*, *Ellora Caves—Sculptures and Architecture*, New Delhi, 1988.

Pathy, T.V., *Ellora: Its Art and Culture*, New Delhi, 1979.

Rajan, K.V. Soundara, *Cave Temples of the Deccan*, New Delhi, 1979.

M.K. Dhavalikar retired as Professor of Archaeology and Director of the Deccan College Post-Graduate and Research Institute, Pune.

The cave temples at Ellora showcase the evolution of Indian sculptural art. They stand testimony both to the mastery of sculptors and the enduring vision of a uniquely Indian aesthetic. Written by an acknowledged expert, this book, part of the *Monumental Legacy* series, provides a succinct overview of the monument's historical background and discusses the development of this World Heritage Site in religious, architectural, and artistic contexts.

Well illustrated with layout plans, maps, and photographs, this volume will be indispensable for general readers and informed tourists vising the site. Students and scholars of history, cultural studies, and art and architecture will also find the work interesting.

'...well researched and sober in its account of the country's heritage ... serious and fascinating ... a splendid showcase of Indian sculptural art.'

—*Sunday Mid-Day*

'The author takes us on a wondrous journey, charting the development of cave architecture and sculpture...'

—*The Mail*

Cover illustration: Cave 10 (Vishwakarma), interior of the chaitya with Buddha image carved over the stupa. Courtesy: American Institute of Indian Studies, Gurgaon.

OXFORD INDIA PAPERBACKS

OXFORD
UNIVERSITY PRESS

www.oup.com

9789388304757